Praise For The Author

"I've had the honour of being able to work closely with Nina Concepcion. One of the things I love most about her is that she walks her talk. She has an uncanny ability to be able to articulate vulnerability and communication (and sales) in such a heart-centred, empowering way."

~ Scott Oldford,
Mentor, Investor & Advisor for Online Businesses

"Nina is passionate about making a difference in people's lives. She takes massive action and does whatever it takes to create success for herself and her clients. So, if you're serious about wanting to be successful in any area of your life or business then speak to Nina and read her book!"

~ Darren Stephens,
International Chairman, Successful Growth Strategies

"Nina is a forward thinker who applies her extensive research and knowledge to developing game changing results. She integrated her methodology with an understanding of our business and the goals of the project."

~ Todd Cooper,
President, Keeping It Neutral Australia (KINA)

The Naked You

GLOBAL
PUBLISHING
GROUP

Global Publishing Group
Australia • New Zealand • Singapore • America • London

A guide to

Embracing Your Imperfections

In Life and Business

The Naked You

Nina Concepcion

DISCLAIMER

All the information, techniques, skills and concepts contained within this publication are of the nature of general comment only and are not in any way recommended as individual advice. The intent is to offer a variety of information to provide a wider range of choices now and in the future, recognising that we all have widely diverse circumstances and viewpoints. Should any reader choose to make use of the information contained herein, this is their decision, and the contributors (and their companies), authors and publishers do not assume any responsibilities whatsoever under any condition or circumstances. It is recommended that the reader obtain their own independent advice.

First Edition 2022

National Library of Australia
Cataloguing-in-Publication entry:

The Naked You, A guide to Embracing Your Imperfections In Life and Business - Nina Concepcion

1st ed.
ISBN: 978-1-925288-98-8 (pbk.)

A catalogue record for this book is available from the National Library of Australia
NATIONAL LIBRARY OF AUSTRALIA

Published by Global Publishing Group
PO Box 517 Mt Evelyn, Victoria 3796 Australia
Email Info@GlobalPublishingGroup.com.au

For further information about orders:
Phone: +61 3 9726 4133

This book is dedicated to my many teachers who have come before me, especially my soul sister, Nic Surma.

Without all of your love and support, I don't know where I'd be today. I'm forever grateful for the immeasurable impact you've each had on my life.

Thank you for believing in me when I didn't.

Thank you for reminding me of my light when I had forgotten.

This book has been made possible because of each of YOU!

xx

Acknowledgements

Nothing one person does is ever truly just created by one person. The creation of this book is a summation of the milestone experiences I have had with people in my life. I believe each and every single person I have encountered in my life has played some type of role. These people I mention here are the ones I would like to give a special thank you to, as they have directly supported me in learning how to first get to know the real me, accepting me, loving me and supporting me in sharing my message.

As I would not physically be here without these two, I feel it is only fitting to firstly thank my parents, Mark and Jenn. Dad, you were a tough dad growing up but your courage and strength has shown me it is never too late to build a meaningful relationship. Thank you for the hard lessons you taught me, as you taught me how to stand my ground and to speak up. Mum, you were my best friend growing up. I didn't understand it back then but it is clear to me now, you were the first person to plant the seed in my mind that the only way to truly heal is to heal myself from the inside out. You also taught me to reflect upon my day and the type of person I was, and to follow my dreams and heart. You have instilled into me many things that today form a big part of the way I think. To both of my parent's partners – Mon and Belle, I am forever grateful for you for bringing out the playful childlike nature in both my parents. I have truly never seen my parents happier than I have seeing them with both of you (instead of with each other haha).

A big thank you to my sister Hayden, for always reminding me to be present, to love, to laugh and to be my crazy self.

My first ever mentor in real estate, Greg was the catalyst into personal development along with being able to create my life on my own terms. From the age of 21, you saw something in me I didn't yet see or even know existed. Thank you for teaching and supporting me in opening up my world, my eyes, my mind and my heart.

I would not be doing the work I do if it wasn't for that fateful day when I met Brendon Burchard back in 2013. I have become a coach, a public speaker and now a published author because this man reflected back at me, exactly just how much one person can impact your entire world.

Now… This man has such a special place in my heart. I will always have so much love and respect for him. Jeffrey Slayter was my first ever spiritual business teacher who taught me that I can be a spiritual entrepreneur. He opened up the door to so many soulful, lifelong relationships and paved the way for thousands of other lightworkers. We wouldn't have the community we do in Australia if it wasn't for Jeff and his work. Thank you for reminding us we are sovereign, complete, loving beings. Kate Gray was also the coach who reflected back to me exactly what I was capable of and supported me in making that a reality! Thank you!

Someone who has come into my life in the last 18 months that has absolutely changed the game of business for me is my current mentor and soon to be business partner Scott Oldford. I am truly a more loving human being because of your influence on me. Thank you for believing in me and reminding me to keep going.

My other mentors through their books, courses, podcasts, videos and other products and services have deeply impacted the quality of life I have today. From my relationships, to the level I am able to contribute, to my wealth, health and state of mind. These include but are not limited to Dr John Demartini, Napoleon Hill, Robin Sharma, Neale Donald Walsch, Brian Tracy, Oprah, Les Brown, T Harv Eker, Arianna Huffington, Louise Hay, Dr Joe Dispenza, Dr Brené Brown, Tony Robbins, Jim Rohn, Bob Proctor, the late Wayne Dyer, Eckhart Tolle, James Redfield, Don Miguel Ruiz, Gary Chapman.

Artists I must thank which have allowed me to cry happy and sad tears, when I've chosen and not chosen to, include but is not limited to Jesse J, Katy Perry and Sara Bareilles.

To all those that have done me harm, I forgive you, I forgive myself, and thank you for playing a part in allowing me to grow stronger.

Thank you to Darren and Jackie Stephens, Kelly, Darlene and the rest of the team at Global Publishing Group. From day one of working with you guys, I always knew you had my back. You were always so willing, helpful and friendly to answering my 500 million questions multiple times a day. The ease and simplicity of the process was truly such a gift along with your support, patience, love and understanding.

Many friends have a special place in my heart but there are three in particular I must acknowledge as they have been pivotal with my happiness and evolution. Nicole Surma, Katie O'Malley and Jayde Jones. Nic, you were my first soul sister I could be crazy spiritual with. Without your love and support, I don't know where I'd be today! I'm forever grateful for the immeasurable impact you've had on my level of belief I have in myself. Thank you for loving me when I didn't know how. Katie, without your friendship, love and support I think I would have had a few psychotic breakdowns by now. You flew in from Bali at the perfect time for the birth of my first child. Lily already knew then, she had to wait for Aunty Katie. You are my dearest sister and words can't describe the love I have for you. You truly are my angel. I love you always. And Jayde, you were my first friend to truly love, accept and fight for me. I know we will be friends and sisters forever. I will always cherish our drunken-alcohol-free all-nighters. I haven't laughed with anyone how I've laughed with you. You have always been a part of my life and always will be.

And of course, lastly my two biggest loves.

Gaz. Thank you for loving and accepting me completely unconditionally. With all my affirmations stuck up around our apartment, I am absolutely sure you thought I was crazy for a few years there, but you supported me anyway. I know you are a natural sceptic but thank you for staying open and always supporting me regardless of your doubts. Thank you for coming to your first ever personal development events with me and watching me speak and present. Thank you for being the first man to fight for me and to actually walk your talk, upholding the integrity that I too stand for. Thank you for being my rock in my life so that I can do the work I love and make the difference I came here to make. I show up that much more fully with my work and clients, because you never fail to show up for me. I love you so much.

And last but definitely not least, my beautiful Lily. You are not old enough to read this yet but one day soon I know you will. Thank you for bringing more joy, happiness, presence and laughter in my life, I didn't even know was possible. You've been the biggest gift that life has given me. Take this book and remember that mum and dad love you, love yourself, and just be you. You are more than enough. The world will learn to accept you, so don't change for the world. Your gift needs sharing! I love you so so so so much.

Contents

Foreword

Dr John Demartini

If I would be asked to recommend a book that will help give people permission to be themselves, *The Naked You* is going to be one of the great ones that will help bring out the magnificence in you.

Having the courage to be yourself is the key and path to authenticity. People can walk on coals, they can do bungee jumps, they can dive out of a plane, and those are metaphors for courage. But the truth is the courage to be yourself is the greatest courage you'll ever have. The courageousness of being authentic to yourself and not minimising yourself to the world and conforming to others. We can't make a difference if we're conforming. We can only make a difference when we're individualised and giving ourselves permission to stand out.

It is time to fully embrace the hero and the villain inside you. We cannot have authenticity until we can embrace both. Embrace both sides of yourself so you don't have to get rid of half of yourself to love yourself. The true authentic you doesn't need anything to get rid of. The true authentic you encompasses all of it.

Don't compare yourself to others. You're not here to subordinate to others, you're not here to live in the shadows of other people, you're not here to conform and minimise yourself to others. You're here to be authentic to you and you can't make the greatest difference if you're not being yourself. You make the greatest difference by living the fullest expression of your unique and evolving hierarchy of values.

Compare instead, your daily actions to your own highest values and dreams and live by priority and delegate all lower priorities off to others. Others who would be inspired to do those things and get paid to also share their authentic selves.

I invite you to experience the journey of embracing your both sides through this book and watch yourself becoming a participant in your own mastery – a master of your destiny more than a victim of your history.

~ Dr John Demartini
International bestselling author of *The Values Factor*

CHAPTER 1

Introduction

CHAPTER 1

Introduction

The Naked You: A guide to living authentically in life and business was initially the name of this book. But I felt that during the time of writing the book "authenticity" is being thrown around a lot. Some people in the spiritual community often use words such as "alignment", "authenticity" and "intuition" as a reason to let fear stop them – spiritual bypassing.

Living authentically…

What does living authentically even mean?

This answer has literally evolved and transformed, probably a dozen times, just in the time of me writing this book. Which is what has made it so challenging finishing it! (Recovering perfectionist right here!)

This is where procrastination and perfectionism has come for me, with writing this book. How do I grasp the infiniteness of our life in one sentence, one paragraph or one book?

The truth is… this book won't give you that ONE answer. It won't encapsulate all that it means to live authentically. But what the book will give you is an insight into my own experiences and what it means to me to live authentically at the time of me writing this.

To me… In a nutshell, living authentically is living in a way that is the most honest and congruent with my values and what matters most to me. It is choosing to listen to my own voice and what is right for me despite the thoughts and opinions of others including and excluding my family and friends. It means truly thinking and feeling for myself. It means having the courage to change direction and focus. It means doing what feels right and what I feel called to do even if people call me crazy. It means taking a leap of faith just because something does or doesn't feel right in my gut. The definition of living authentically means to be open to the definition changing from each moment and each phase of my life and everything in between. It means questioning everything and being discerning about my own discernment. It means being open to even more depth, truth and clarity, even if it means me being wrong, confused and feeling lost. It is allowing the older version of me to die so that the new version of myself can be born.

Living authentically means growth. Which means that what once felt right, may not feel right anymore or may not feel right at another stage of my life. As the famous saying goes, what got you here, won't get you there.

Living authentically means having the courage to let go – let go of all you know, all you think to be, and all you think and believe to be true. Then starting again.

I am constantly faced with the question – am I willing to let go of what doesn't matter to let in what does? Am I more concerned with being right or being truly deeply happy? Often what I am holding onto is just my ego, just a habit, just what I think I "should" be doing.

To me living authentically means taking action regardless of your fears. And not taking action is in itself an action. How can we instead, consciously choose our actions? Rather than avoiding making a decision all together and wondering why we feel stuck.

To embrace our imperfections is what it means to me to live authentically. In order to finish this book I truly had to exercise embracing my imperfections. This is the reason why I decided to change the subtitle of this book.

How could I embrace more of my imperfections? How could I love more? How can I love myself and others deeper? This book has been my practice in doing just that. There is nothing like embracing your imperfections by climbing the mountain of writing an entire book!

This is what I kept in mind when writing and everything I do – this is ONE part of my legacy. Not THE legacy. This is PART of the masterpiece not THE masterpiece. There is no perfection. Only progress and growth. How can you take this into your life and business? How can you stop putting pressure on yourself to have that one book, that one course, that one program, that one relationship, completely define who you are and your value?

Growing up I always had this deep sense that something was missing...
Like a PART of me was missing... Maybe many parts of me. I just couldn't figure out what it was or even how to find it... But of course life led me in the direction to find it. I just needed to be open and to have the courage to trust myself and take action.

This book will uncover my story of being aware of my masks of who I am not, to continually discover what matters, and how I have and continue to learn how to embrace, love and share the unique expression of me. The beautiful, the ugly, the crazy, the weird, the different. All of it.

I will be giving suggestions in this book including questions to journal and meditate upon, along with songs to listen to and movies to watch that have supported me in my journey.

This will support you to integrate, reflect and discover more about what currently drives you and whether or not that still serves you. To get the absolute most out of this book. I HIGHLY recommend journaling on the questions. If not while you read the book, then journal on it after reading the book.

I will be your guide and coach. This means I will not always just give you the answer. Like the old proverb goes, it's more empowering to teach a man how to fish than to give them a fish.

I also interviewed some of my most influential mentors for their point of view on this topic including Dr John Demartini, Jeffrey Slayter and Scott Oldford. Listen to the stories, ask yourself the questions, look for your own answers, and dig for your own gold. It is up to you and you alone to define what living authentically, embracing your imperfections, living in alignment and what living a purposeful life means to you.

At the time of writing this book I built the Institute of Conscious Sales as a "Conscious Sales" Coach who supports ambitious heart-centred coaches in building their coaching from 0 to 6 figures, through organic social media (no ads). I help people see, embrace and share just how amazing they are and how to monetise their gifts to amplify their impact in the world.

Being your guide and coach throughout this book, I encourage you to make a decision now if you are willing and open to receiving. As I give you suggestions throughout the book, take what resonates, get curious when you are triggered, remember there is no perfection and lean into opening your heart.

This is my truth and definitely not an absolute truth of what is. The one thing I am sure of is that my truth will continue to evolve. I invite you in reading this book, to take what resonates and leave the rest. To ask yourself, what does living authentically mean to you?

As much as it's my hope that I can impact, inspire and awaken at least ONE person the same way my mentors have empowered me, I also just trust that in whomever hands this book lands, you will get exactly what you need to get out of it. Although I feel the energy and impact of this book, I write this to you practicing nonattachment and putting my ego to the side. I'm just listening, trusting, surrendering, and taking action, in the same way I have learnt to live and be guided by my life and my business.

I am a vehicle for this msg. I am one of many vehicles. Travelling far and wide to reach as many souls that are searching, ready and willing.
You may not like what I have to say. At times you may cry, laugh, get angry or even triggered. There will likely be concepts that challenge you, your way of thinking and your identity. I'm just reminding you it is up to you whether or not you want to dive deep and how deep you dive. It is up to you what you decide to take on, try on and take off, or just leave it in the book.

I speak my truth at the time of me writing this book and I also understand and accept my truth continues to evolve and adapt. This all starts with a willingness to see that maybe just maybe, I'm wrong. Maybe my thoughts are wrong. Maybe my feelings are just conditioned behaviours and habits. Maybe yours are too?

A more accurate choice of words is probably "disempowering" as opposed to "wrong". So when I say/write the word "wrong", this is really what I mean. What I love about the word wrong is that for me it really allows me to question my ego. Because when I want to be right, and I realise that's all I am really holding onto you, I realise exactly why it's necessary to let a belief or thought go.

If a thought or feeling disempowers me, for me it is worth looking at, deconstructing and adopting a new thought or belief. This is a place I encourage you to get curious about within your own journey. Not just when reading this book but in life.

This is the premise of all transformation. A shift in awareness and mindset.

And if we are unwilling to look at where we could potentially be wrong. We are missing opportunities for growth.

To me it doesn't even matter if I'm "right" or "wrong". Rather does this empower or disempower me. All life is perspective. And if truth lies somewhere between different perspectives, and if the perspective I choose dictates my life, rather than choosing to have the right opinion, I choose to have an empowering mindset.

Yes I may be wrong…
Yes I may be right…
I may be somewhere in between.
Your truth may also be somewhere in between for you to discover…

It's up to you to discern your own truth. I believe things now I didn't once believe. And I had absolute beliefs I no longer believe.

My truth is to write this because as much as it's confronting, uncomfortable and scary, this is part of my process of surrendering to what my intuition is calling me, guiding me to do, express and be.

Your truth is always entirely completely up to you. Whether it's a book, a friend, a movie, a conversation, a teacher or mentor, our beliefs ARE GOING to be challenged. Are we willing to have an open belief system? Are we willing to be open minded? Whilst at the same time discerning our own truth and deeply trusting our own decisions… That's when no one else's opinion will matter more than yours and frankly, no other opinion will trigger you because you know there is no truth in it. As Dr John Demartini says, we only ever get triggered when there is some level of truth, something for us that we are unwilling to face.

Regardless of how your journey plays out…

I acknowledge you and honour you. For you to have picked up this book tells me that you are someone who is deeply committed to your growth and being your most authentic self. You also desire more love in your life. You don't just have a commitment to yourself, but to those you love and serve. And this is the road least taken. You may even be called to create a new road, a road NOT yet taken. And that takes courage and strength.

For that I thank you. Although I may never completely grasp the impact you have and are making, what I am sure of is that you ARE making a difference and an impact. The same way that my mentors will likely never grasp how much my life has changed because of them. Never underestimate the power of one question, one call, listening to one person, or smiling at a stranger. We are all making an impact.

I feel this truth in every core of my being.

If you are here with me, you are a reflection of me. There is something within me that resonates within you. The same way my teachers reflect something in me.

For you, I am grateful.

Thank you for being you. Thank you for doing the internal work, and taking the action. Thank you for the difference you are making including what you are and aren't aware you are doing. Thank you for being here. If you are like me, and you like to also learn and integrate with videos you can get *The Naked You: Online Course* here www.TheNakedYouBook.com/Resources where I go into more depth about these topics.

And I am excited to have this journey with you. While I write this, I feel you… and know that you're here with me, as I am with you, while you read this.

~ Listen to *Masterpiece* by Jesse J ~

Not Just Words

What that I believe
My words conveys
Is the simplicity and love
Of a simple gaze

Not just the meaning
But the feeling too
Of something we connect with
From me to you

Words that come flowing out of my heart
Seems to flow out from the moment I start

For me it's a release
A piece of me
To get my mind straight
And to be able just to be

To clear my head and the thoughts going on
To express my feelings to sometimes not prolong

To sometimes remember this feeling of bliss
Or to express and release
What I wish to dismiss

A part of me
I have learnt to embrace
That maybe it can help you
Create your own space

In this crazy world we live in each day
To have even one moment of presence
To experience a possibility of a path
To a new way

~ Nina Concepcion

CHAPTER 2

Intention

CHAPTER 2

Intention

While you're reading, listen not just to the words, but to what your feelings are saying… What your soul is whispering. What your body responds to. What brings tears to your eyes. Be open to the experience of this book so that you can take it into your life. One of the things I love about reading is that it requires our full attention and presence. Unlike watching a movie or listening to something, where we can still multitask. For that reason if you are listening to the audio I also encourage you to purchase the book because there will be moments that can only be found in reading, while there are also moments that will happen while listening.

When we give something our entire presence, we can open up the space to receive gifts we wouldn't otherwise have the awareness to notice or accept.

For that, I wish for you to have the best possible opportunity to receive all that you desire to call in.

But like anything in life we choose to grow in, it requires our focus, attention and presence.

One of my amazing mentors Scott Oldford says if you look at the areas of your life that you have the best results – career, money, relationships, health – it's the area you have given the most time, energy, presence and focus. Therefore the areas that you feel are lacking are the areas you haven't given much of your attention to.

In order to get a new level of results in your life, whatever that may be, shift your attention and focus.

My guess is that you are called to this book without knowing why OR you are clear that finding your authentic self and embracing all you are is a priority for you right now. So with the time we have together, I encourage you to give yourself the gift of presence, love and attention towards inquiring into the quality of life you are living.

Simply by making that decision to consciously decide what to focus your attention on, your life will begin to transform.

There is only so much that words can express. I like to use the analogy of sex because the majority of us understand it! Plus it's funny :) Ok, so how do you describe to a virgin what great sex feels like? Words don't really grasp the feeling of the experience! So as I write this book, not only am I expressing myself in words, but I'm also pouring out my heart, soul and love to transmit the energy and experience for those of you ready and willing to receive it. Once we can open ourself up to the experience, the words make sense. But if we just try to understand logically, we will never really grasp the experience.

It's like when I speak to my mentors. Before I even finish asking my question, their presence alone allows me to see the answer!

Funny how energy works! ;)

At the same time… when we allow ourselves to be truly open and present…

An incredibly powerful experience can occur…

This is an experience of when a book completely changes our life.

Although I do not have that expectation for you as the reader, I am sharing all of me in a way that there is that possibility to transmute my life-changing moments here in order to support you to have your own.

Speaking to thousands of people globally… I have seen first hand the power of not only hearing and feeling other people's stories but also sharing my own…

I share mine with you, to encourage you to face your own stories and to inspire you to share your own. This means facing your light and your darkness. It means facing what you are proud of but also your imperfections.

It's so powerful when we come across a text that awakens a remembering within us.

A knowingness.
A calmness.
A peace.

A feeling of – OMFG that's exactly how I've been feeling but didn't know how to articulate it until now.

Or a feeling of – OMFG yes that's the answer I've been looking for without even knowing how to ask the question!

Or a feeling of – OMFG this is exactly what I've been craving, looking for and needing and didn't even realise it!!! How often have we said to ourselves *that's exactly what I needed to hear/read today*?!

There are many texts that have done that for me. I believe it comes down to a combination of the essence of the text itself, me being open and ready to receive it and slowing down enough to be willing to look for your own answers, meaning and truth.

Some of these texts have supported me in my journey that I would love to acknowledge include *The Four Agreements*, *A Leader Without a Title*, *Think and Grow Rich*, *The Conversations With God series*, *Man's Search For Meaning*, *Levels of Energy*, *Light Is The New Black*, *Girl Stop Apologising* and *The Gene Keys*.

My hope is that this book will support you in an awakening and remembering of who you are and who you came here to be. Not necessarily what you came here to do, although that is a by-product of remembering.

My intention for this book is to inspire you, the reader, to realise that perfection is the death of progress and that you can live a life beyond your wildest dreams.

But you must deeply desire it, act upon it, take self-responsibility and trust yourself more than what society and your loved ones say you "should be doing". Perfection is not an excuse to not take action. You do not help anyone if you are stuck in your own insecurities.

This book was created to support you in closing the gap from where you are to where you want to be. It is a constant journey. One thing I am sure of, is that through practicing vulnerability every day, we can reach inner fulfilment and true connection sooner rather than later.

> ~ Take a moment now to journal or meditate on your intention for this book ~

Not only will you attract the answer in this book, but also your everyday life.

QUESTIONS
- Why did you purchase this book?
- Why did you decide to read this book?
- What are you seeking and calling in to your life right now?

If you are curious about the work I do with coaches and entrepreneurs you can claim your free gift at www.TheNakedYouBook.com/Resources

Love Yourself

Love for yourself can only really be felt by you
No one can ever take it away
Because it's not possible for them to do

People and circumstances can expand it and shine a light
to what already is
Or it can reveal the absence
You can choose not to continue to dismiss

Are you seeking inside you,
Or the illusion of what's outside
When you seek inside you
There's really nothing and nowhere for you to hide

There is where you'll find real love
And a peace no one can explain
There you can find gratitude for everything
And all the levels of your pain

Have the courage to go forth
and to venture deep within
It's not as unknown as you may think
It's just where everything starts again to begin

~ Nina Concepcion

~ Journal/Meditate on your intention
for our time together ~

CHAPTER 3

In-Perfection

CHAPTER 3

In-Perfection

Imperfection or I'm Perfection?

I will just start by claiming yes… I am a recovering perfectionist. Key word… recoverING. It is and probably always will be a process…

As a preteen I remember growing up wishing I could be someone else.

If I was prettier, more popular, had lighter skin, a pointier nose… then maybe I would fit in. That maybe I would be loved. Maybe then I would feel like I belong.

I seemed to just always think *If I was them I wouldn't have the problems I have. I wouldn't be insecure. I would love myself more. Other people would love me too.*

The truth that I didn't know back then is that everyone has these challenges. Everyone has insecurities. Even the most beautiful women I have ever met. I was NOT alone in feeling this way.

I have spent (or invested) a good portion of my life trying to uncover who I am. A deep longing to discover parts of me I felt were missing.

When I was younger I found myself feeling lost, alone and vulnerable.

I found myself becoming more and more confused about my life and about who I was.

Almost out of nowhere, but as if perfectly timed, the nightmares started…

Recurring nightmares of the same thing happening over and over. I became increasingly moody and angry. I thought maybe it was just my new hormones coming into my teen years.

But the nightmares persisted.

The recurring nightmare became more and more vivid. That's exactly what I thought they were. Nightmares.

As they became more vivid, it started to feel like… like… a memory… I started to see my younger cousins in my dreams too… I was slowly seeing a picture, then a movie with more characters, more colour, more sounds.

I couldn't ignore it any longer. My intuition told me I needed to ask my younger cousin who was in my dream. I thought to myself… if she remembers it.. Then I know that they aren't nightmares at all.

So the 12 (or so) year old me… Waited for the next family gathering so that I could ask my younger cousin about these dreams.

The moment I opened my mouth in that tiny room at my uncle's house… I watched the blood drain from her young innocent face.

She went into panic mode…!

Nina, you can't tell anyone. It will break up our entire family!

THAT was the moment I realised that it was possible for your mind to block something out of your memory as if it never happened. I had unconsciously repressed memories of sexual abuse as a child, now resurfacing through my dreams. THIS was a part of me that was missing! My memory…!

Instantly the walls in that already small room began to shrink smaller and smaller. It was a fact. It was undeniable now. I had been sexually abused by a distant family member. It was as if time slowed down and all I could hear was my breath and my heart beating.

Side Note: Throughout the rest of this book I will not continue to refer to that experience as "abuse" but rather my Turning Point Experience (TPE) as I feel the word "abuse" is disempowering, which is the complete opposite of the intention for this book.

I questioned what the next right step was. My cousin and I were both still so young, so innocent, still pre-puberty. I wasn't sure what to do so I allowed her fear to overwhelm me and I agreed to keep this our little secret.

It was the first time in my life I tried to sweep an issue under the rug. To try and move on, and forget, and pretend it never happened. Little did I know how difficult this would be for me.

Over the following weeks and months I went from being sad and moody… to falling into depression… to being angry and physically harming myself.

I was spiralling further and further down…

Then I was confronted with a harsh and scarier truth… Did I have the courage to face it?

What I didn't realise, is the moment we speak something out loud, we have already begun to confront it. I had already started to face it! But I knew more challenges lay ahead. As much as I tried to ignore it, the pain and anger just got stronger and stronger… I tried to ignore it for as long as I could… Until I couldn't anymore…

When we share our story we give others the space to think about their own life. We automatically put ourselves into our own lives and look for a similar situation in our own lives.

I believe other people's stories can show us the strength of feeling the depths of our emotions that we may not even be aware of. From ugly crying to absolutely pissing ourselves laughing. Stories capture our attention and force us, in a way to be aware of and acknowledge how we feel about a topic

I met the first person to ever show me the power of story one day at school camp. That day was called Reflection Day. I don't remember her name but I am forever grateful for her sharing her story that day.

She reflected back to me the need to also speak my truth, but this time to the most important people who needed to know how I felt… my parents. I was about to do the scariest thing that I had ever done.

I was tired of blaming my parents for not knowing how I was feeling. I was tired of having screaming matches with my parents just because I was angry. I was tired of being angry with life. I was tired of cutting my wrist to escape the emotional pain. I was tired of feeling misunderstood.

The moment I told my mum, I was finally able to start letting go of the pain... As the famous saying goes, a burden shared is a burden halved. I could literally feel the pain falling off me, like shedding a layer of old skin.

I started to truly accept what had happened to me. Without even realising it at the time... I was learning how to love myself through the pain. I was learning how to hold myself and know that I was ok. It wasn't until years and decades later that I began to learn how to embrace the uniqueness of my story.

I was, however most importantly, finally starting to heal. I removed the first mask in my life I had ever worn. The mask of pretending I was ok when I wasn't. The mask of sweeping my emotions under the rug. The mask of not being able to be me and speak my truth. The mask of thinking *no one understands me*, in order to keep me hidden from the world.

~ Listen to *Rise Up* by Andra Day ~

Asking questions begins the process of us opening up to the answers we seek. However, when we attract something new into our life, many of us tend to also question our ability to do something new, our imperfections, our value, our self-worth... If you want transformation, you need to be willing to be open, to let new information in and become a better receiver.

~ Journal on the questions below ~

QUESTIONS

- How good am I at receiving compliments? About the things you have and haven't accepted about myself?
- Do I deflect by throwing out another random compliment just so that I won't feel uncomfortable? Or do I genuinely appreciate it, letting it land, allowing myself to feel it and looking that person in the eye and sincerely thanking them for reflecting back what I also know about myself?

It is exhausting keeping up with the facade of being perfect.

Even when you are not conscious of it. As humans it is natural for us to identify with our results, our success, our wealth, our impact. But that is not who we are to our core.

There have been times that I have been broke, in debt, living off $20 a day and been incredibly happy and unattached. And there have been times that I have had more than enough money and felt unhappy and broken. This is proof that our happiness does not lie in what we have, but who we feel and believe we are.

When everything falls away what do you hold onto? What are you willing to let go of?

Perfection has become an old friend that wants to connect every so often. I understand we were very close at one point but I am learning to love her from afar. Perfection is an illusion. At some level we think to ourselves – *Once you are perfect you will be happy. Once you become a bestselling author people will love you. Once you are rich people will respect you.* We are setting ourselves up to fail by setting those expectations for ourselves. Not only do we fail at the destination but also on the journey.

Through the journey of personal, spiritual and business development I continue to learn to love myself. I am learning to embrace my imperfections that little bit more each day, week and month.

Although I am far from perfect, and I'm constantly uncovering new fears, insecurities and imperfections to embrace at a deeper level…

I don't ever wish to be anyone but who I am anymore. Because this would mean losing everyone I love and my connection with them. I would not be the person I am now without them. So why would I change who I am? That's not to say I don't constantly want to improve who I am and be a more loving human, but unlike two decades ago, I am no longer trying to run away from being me.

I deeply love the people in my life and what they mean to me. I love that they completely accept me for me and vice versa. To really experience love and acceptance is priceless. This is what I'd love for you – the reader…

THIS is why today, I choose to be vulnerable. This is the reason I choose to share my challenges. This is the reason why I'm constantly sharing my mistakes. My imperfections.

I believe… that gone are the days that we look at someone and think "Wow that's so amazing. I could never be like her." We are craving more authenticity and realness in a society now that encourages us to promote only the best parts of our lives. We all know of someone who looks like they have it all together on social media, but are really struggling internally.

We are becoming smarter as a species. More intuitive. We can smell when someone is being fake and insincere.

We crave to see idols, celebrities, mentors, leaders and guides who are not trying to be perfect, but are willing to be real and raw with us. And against all odds they have also managed to come out the other end and triumphed. I know I crave this. Do you?

I am not inspired by the person who seems to be lucky. By the person who was born into luck. I am inspired by those who are just like me and inspire me to believe that despite my challenges, past and insecurities, if I don't let those things stop me, that they won't!

The underdog has always been inspiring. We don't resonate as much with people who seem to achieve success too easily because we think that means that for us it's unattainable and impossible. We start to question, *why didn't it come 'easily' to us*?

Rather than striving for perfection… find joy in each moment instead. Including the challenging and difficult times. When we stop putting that expectation on ourselves, when we stop thinking that we are a lesser version of ourselves and we release the guilt of who we think we should be or what we think we should be doing. We stop beating ourselves up for being perfectly imperfect.

When we can learn to love and accept ourselves exactly where we are, with kindness, patience and understanding, we can start to tap into what it is we so desperately seek. This does not mean we won't still want to thrive and achieve, but we can learn to become unattached to the outcome, the deadline and that feeling we think is only attainable once we hit that goal.

One of my good friends Aaron Mashano says that he doesn't strive for perfection. Because once something is perfect there is no more room for growth.

So rather than striving for perfection, why not strive for growth?

Perfection can imply there is only one correct way of doing something and that every other way is incorrect or wrong.

That's like saying one type of butterfly is perfect and another is not.

It was through my experience of that TPE that I was able to stand strong in not giving into peer pressure. However there was still that little girl inside me that just wanted to fit in. I just wanted to be loved. I just wanted to feel like one of the cool kids and wanted to feel accepted.

I just knew I wasn't willing to make the sacrifice I saw people around me making.

It's why growing up, I never took drugs, smoked or did anything "too reckless". I was never going to put myself in a situation again where I felt I could be taken advantage of.

I am far from perfect, but I knew I didn't want to necessarily be what others wanted or expected me to be either.

For the entrepreneur… Why you?

Unconsciously we ask ourselves questions like…

Am I good enough?
Why me?
If it's not perfect does that mean my work is not worthy?

This is something we ALL ask and feel but I'll speak directly to those who give of themselves in a way that we feel as if we are sharing our heart literally to anyone and everyone. This is what happens when we step into the courage to share our gifts in a massive way. I've literally invested hundreds and thousands of dollars into my business at this moment in time. Initially I thought it was for me and what I wanted. But as I was tested, as I fell down and I was beaten and felt defeated, as I questioned everything, as I felt like giving up… what made me continue moving forward was nothing more than a calling, a need, a pull. Something I could ignore sometimes but would always eventually get too strong that I had no other choice but to follow where I was being guided.

So let's talk about being good enough…

When we are creating a course, a program, a book… anything… How do we know if it's good enough?

Many of us ask ourselves. Why should we teach this? Why should we write about that? Why should I share my message of ABC when there are already other amazing leaders, teachers, speakers and authors on this topic? But the truth is…

Only YOU can express it with your unique energetic blueprint.

This is something I've had to remind myself as I write this book.

I can find inspiration in many books, documentaries, conversations, courses, events and films. What makes me so special I ask myself? But when I am drawn to one MORE book on a topic that I have already read about... does it make the last book I read any less valuable or meaningful?

No. If anything it actually reinforces and adds value to each other.

Everyone expresses themselves differently. Everyone has their own lens of their own experience. Everyone communicates differently. Everyone can describe the same experience with different words. The same painting with a different perspective.

This is exactly why the more we embrace ALL of who we are, the more we can make the difference we came here to make. We were not designed or destined to be exactly the same as another.

Someone else's value doesn't make anyone else, less valuable.

The sun is no more important than the air we breathe.

So what are some of the signs of when we have fallen into perfection-itis!
1. When we procrastinate
2. Analysis paralysis – When we take no action and just get caught in a loop of over analysing and thinking
3. When we feel overwhelmed it's normally due to a lack of accountability, direction, strategy and action.

So how do we beat it!? These are the same symptoms when we have imposter syndrome so the cure is also the same!

"We beat imposter syndrome
when we shift our attention from self to service"
~ Nina Concepcion

Imposter syndrome is something many of my clients experience in the pursuit of making a bigger difference. My quote above sums it up simply. When we are focused on ourselves we are focused on what we don't know, how much more we have to learn. But when someone is in need, we focus on what we do know and how we can help. It's all about a shift in perception. A shift in our mindset.

While writing this book, I continually asked myself, how can I express and share my heart in a way that I can be proud of how I showed up? Because I have released the expectation that this book is the be all and end all, of my best work. As long as I continue to grow, so will the potency of my work. But as I share with my clients all the time, just because you're still learning, it doesn't mean you can't inspire and help those who are earlier in the journey than you. Those you help could literally just be you, yesterday. You're never too old to learn and you're never too young to teach.

So how can we lean into ourselves more? How can we embrace more of who we are? The beautiful and the ugly. The light and the shade?

How can we step more fully into the versions of ourselves bursting to be born?

~ Journal on the questions below ~

QUESTIONS
- How can I strengthen my belief in my ability to learn and improve?
- How willing and committed am I to my mission and my message?
- What matters more, my insecurities or the impact I am here to make?
- Who do I know or who can I seek out that will help me implement a proven strategy that I can leverage?

Do I have the courage to accept myself for all that I am?

God (or universe, the divine, whatever you would like to place here),
Grant me the serenity to accept the things I cannot change, courage to change the things I can, and wisdom to know the difference.
~ Serenity Prayer

It took me years…

To believe I was beautiful.

To believe that I didn't "do" anything to deserve being sexually abused.

To believe how amazing I am and the potential I have.

To embrace and learn to love my crazy witch cackle of a laugh.

To stop feeling super-insecure about my stretch marks on my thighs I've had since I was 12.

To not judge myself for my small boobs.

To embrace my heritage as a Filipino (there is still much more for me to learn and to explore).

To believe I was worthy of love.

To believe I was worthy of receiving and abundance.

It took me years and it's all still a work in progress…

Of course a lot of this was and is internal work, taking action even when I was scared and believing something else was possible for my life… But something else that truly helped me was and is having loved ones who loved parts of me that I was still learning to love within myself. If they could accept me, why couldn't I?

I am accepting more and more, that I'MPERFECT just the way I am. Imperfection for me means being perfect in my own way. It doesn't mean I don't make mistakes. I don't mean I don't still strive for growth. It means there is no need to feel guilty for not being what society says or thinks I should be. As long as I trust my intuition, I will know what is right for me. Others may say I am wrong, but I will stay true to me.

IMPERFECT = I'm Perfect = I Am Perfect

As are you!

Your imperfections create who you're relevant to
[your audience and clients].
~ Scott Oldford

CHAPTER 4

Courage To Believe

CHAPTER 4

Courage to believe

*Courage in its original definition comes from the word Cur. Cur means heart. It means **to tell the story of who you are with your whole heart.** Courage to be imperfect. Having the compassion to be kind to yourselves first then to others, because as it turns out we can't practice compassion with other people if we cannot treat ourselves kindly.*
~ Brené Brown

Six years of high school and I still didn't know what I wanted to do with my life. I was unhappy with what I was doing at university, so during my three-month break I applied for a three-month receptionist role. Instead I was offered a minimum 12 month sales role. The complete opposite to what I was looking for.

Are you willing to be open to the unexpected?

When I was offered this job, at the time it was a really difficult decision. I had a bunch of reasons why I was hesitant. One, I had no sales experience. Two, at the time I cared more about what other people thought of me than what I thought of me. I was so used to seeking a lot of opinions from others as opposed to really listening to my own thoughts. Half the people in my life said I would do well because I am a people person and the other half said I would be eaten alive.

Not to mention, I also decided to get lingual braces… Which are braces on the inner side of your teeth, which meant that people couldn't see my braces but it caused me to have a really bad lisp. So I had all of these insecurities thinking *no one is going to want to buy a house from a young Asian with braces and a lisp who looks like she's 18!*

Are you allowing your insecurities, fears and imperfections stop you?

It was the first time in my life where I really had to choose between something that I was comfortably unhappy in… with venturing into the unknown for the potential for more.

Ultimately I decided to take a leap of faith because I knew that I wasn't happy or enjoying what I was studying at university. I knew that was never going to be what I would do for the rest of my life.

It ended up taking me nine months to make a commission in real estate. I then became 2nd in Charge in my office, I was promoted to Sales Executive, I became the 4th highest sales person in the company by my 3rd quarter, I started training all the new staff and began the discussions of opening up an office with my boss. I bought my own home and started travelling solo.

What I realised was….

I could really just be me.

That I could honour my own values.

That I had the courage to walk my own path.

I found the courage to honour my integrity (as opposed to being manipulative).

I was actually able to build a successful career in real estate BECAUSE I was so different to what people expected me to be. This idea and paradigm shift of being authentically yourself in sales, was the seedling of what years later, I would term "Conscious Sales".

Do you have the courage to be different?

Of course it was hard. Of course I felt like giving up multiple times…

I wouldn't know I had the courage to do what I did if I didn't give myself the chance.

Until I saw myself do it, I never truly believed with my whole being, that I was worthy or able to do a good job. For months I doubted my ability. For months I questioned if I was good enough. For months I questioned if I had made the right decision.

But I chose to have the courage to believe! To believe that something else was possible for me.

Borrow my belief in you until your belief takes over.
~ Les Brown

My boss at the time was my first ever mentor. I would have definitely given up without his support and guidance. It is imperative that you surround yourself with people who have more belief and courage than you! By the power of osmosis you will believe more for yourself simply by being in their company.

We need to have the courage to ask for help.

I was so glad I hadn't allowed the many insecurities, fears and excuses around my imperfections stop me from giving something new a go. This experience was a pivotal moment and milestone in gaining the experience, courage, resilience and values in building my own business. If I let fear stop me, you probably would not have this book in your hands.

> ~ Take a moment here to stop, reflect and journal on anything that has resonated, taught or inspired you ~

QUESTIONS
- How can I not let my fears and insecurities stop me?
- How can I care more about my own opinions over others' opinions of me?
- How willing am I to try something new, for the potential for more?

When I finally thought I had my life figured out…
Once again the universe had other plans!

It was yet again time to remove another layer of who I am not. Or at least, who I no longer was. I thought real estate was hard… Selling something for someone else is 100x easier than selling what you have created yourself! Why? Because part of this process seems to be that ALL your insecurities and imperfections rise to the surface for you to work through! The funny thing is as much as it sounds like a pain in the ass, if someone HAD told me this sooner, I still would have done it! (I would have just hired help faster!) I believe it's the price we pay for making a bigger impact.

So there I was… Completely unaware of what was about to happen.

I was at the peak of my career in real estate when I was invited by my team leader to go to a personal development event. His wife was suddenly unable to attend (synchronicity much?). This event changed the course of my life.

I remember as I sat there in the front row, listening to multiple speakers, I noticed I was one of the youngest people there wondering why there weren't more younger people at these events! As I listened to speaker after speaker I was increasingly inspired until one man walked onto the stage with more love and presence than I had ever seen.

I had no idea who he was before that but within a couple of minutes of listening to him speak, I just had this massive wave and I thought *OMG. I have never felt so alive, so much so that I felt dead up until this point.* Years later I found this quote:

The *two best days of your life is the day that you were born, and the day that you knew why.*
~ Mark Twain

THIS day was the "day I knew why". As I sat there listening to him share his story, I just sat there crying and crazily writing nonstop in my notebook. The main thing that I wrote down was that I was going to be a coach, a speaker and an author. I was going to impact the world by sharing what I knew, what I've experienced and what I've learned so that I could make other people's lives better.

That man I heard speak was the one and only Brendon Burchard!

Many of us now know who Brendon Bouchard is today. There were only a couple hundred people in that room and most of us didn't know who he was. Today, he's one of the world's most followed influencers on social media. In my mind, he was already changing the world then! I have been a lifelong fan ever since! I built up the courage to walk up to him, tell him how much his speech impacted me and got a photo with him :D

I didn't know at the time that I was going to birth the Institute of Conscious Sales. However, I knew that I wanted to do something with regard to the personal development influential space. I just knew that I wanted to do what Brendon was doing.

One person can make all the difference! For me this was Brendon. You too can be this person for someone else.

I wanted to impact just one person the same way that Brendon had impacted me. I just didn't know how or even where to start.

The next day, I went back to real estate. My plan was that in five years (when I was financially free) that is when I would pursue my new aspirations.

That five-year plan became two weeks!!

There IS no perfect time.

I went back to work and I literally felt like my soul was dying. I just could not be there anymore. I couldn't believe how completely different it felt being back at work. It reminds me of when you catch up with a best friend that you haven't seen in years, and you realise that you no longer have anything in common with them. That's what it felt like!

But it was just a few days after the event!!!! Definitely a WTF moment!

I was no longer in alignment with what once served me. I had learnt the lesson I needed to learn.

Something I love to tell people is that in the week that I was building up the courage to give my resignation, I was headhunted by two other real estate agencies. Keep in mind, I applied to these agencies back two years ago when I had no sales experience!

I truly believe that when you decide you want more for your life, the universe will test you and tempt you right when you are about to make a decision to see if you want what you truly say you want, or if you are going to sacrifice your dreams for immediate gratification.

I took a deep breath and said no to those other opportunities. I had my eye on a new vision. Those new roles would give me PART of what I am looking for, but ultimately I knew I would outgrow that too.

Do you have the courage to say no to opportunities that only offer short-term wins?

So, that's when I decided to leave real estate and pursue my new dream of being a coach, a speaker, and an author.

It was almost eight years ago that I left real estate. It was 2013 when I met Brendon. It took me almost seven years to become a six-figure income earner as a coach and over five years to have finished writing my book! I'm finally now getting my first book published. The one that you have in your hands! :D 🖤

Just another reminder that even if it can take close to a decade for some dreams to come true, it's still worth it. You just need to decide, would it be worth it for you? Remember that although my dreams are coming true now, many of my dreams had already come true in the pursuit of THIS dream. In the pursuit of my dreams, I have discovered something more powerful… The journey, the people… and myself.

All because I had the courage to desire more for my life, to take action, and to venture into the unknown.

Courage is a muscle!!! If you don't use it you lose it!

The very first thing I needed was to have the courage to trust myself, my ability to make my own decisions and to think for myself. Next, I needed to not only build my own belief in myself, but also surround myself with mentors and peers who had a stronger belief than I did, so that my belief through the power of osmosis alone supported my belief in getting stronger.

Eventually through persistence, practice, action and mentorship, over time, my belief in my own abilities became solid that there isn't anything anyone could say to break it.

~ Journal on the questions below ~

QUESTIONS
- When an opportunity presents itself to you, do you exercise the courage to believe?
- Do you exercise the courage to believe in something bigger than your current circumstances?
- Do you have the courage to dream big?
- Are you surrounding yourself with empowering relationships that support you in building your own beliefs and confidence in yourself?

Are you willing to choose being authentic over being liked?

Our ability to be honest with ourselves about exactly what is going on with us and how we are feeling, dictates our ability to feel free.

How do you hold space for yourself? Can you feel the subtleties of unease? Do you give yourself the time and space to allow deeper buried conditioned feelings to surface for healing?

Do you have the courage to be with the pain?

Being honest with ourselves is one of the hardest things needed for our growth and transformation. Why? Because once we see the truth we cannot unsee. We cannot continue to be in denial once we admit the truth.

Think back to a relationship that deep down you knew was not good for you. Looking back, how long did you know before you actually admit it to yourself? It's like once we finally express it, and the truth is out, we cannot put it back in the bottle. Most of us lie to ourselves to avoid taking responsibility so that we don't need to take any action or make a change. We just hope that that relationship will somehow get better without confronting how we are really feeling.

I have seen time and time again, that either you make a change or eventually the change will be made FOR you! I believe that the universe has a grand plan for our lives, and the more we resist it the harder it becomes. This all begins with self-honesty.

With self-honesty comes building self-awareness of your thoughts, feelings and actions... Allowing yourself to be seen and heard... and ultimately feeling accepted, first by yourself, then by others.

So then how are some ways we can start being more honest with ourselves?

This is a muscle like everything else in life. It takes time and practice. I honestly wish someone had given me this advice when I was younger when I didn't have the awareness to ask high quality questions.

Here are some ways to build your level of self-honesty in order of difficulty:
1. Journaling
2. Spending time in nature or meditation
3. Speaking to someone you love and trust

4. Hiring a coach/mentor/guide you trust and resonate with who is
    further along the path than you

Journaling was the first tool I ever discovered that helped me build my
ability to be honest with myself. When I fell into depression after my
repressed memories surfaced, the one thing I did all the time was write
in my journal, write poetry and listen to songs that I resonated with.

I feel that we learn how to hold space for ourselves when we are having
an internal dialogue with ourselves. We also cannot multitask while
speaking to ourselves.

Initially I would just write anything that came to mind. Word vomiting
on the page. Venting however I was feeling. I would often write just
because I didn't know how to articulate how I was feeling. Through
writing I would start to figure it out.

When I broke the news to my mum with what had happened to me, I
actually told her through a letter. I couldn't bring myself to speak the
words out loud because I was crying so much and it felt too painful to
even speak. I wish I knew where that letter was! I would love to read
and viscerally remember the courage it took for me to write it. It's not
something you think about at the time, to keep a letter like that, but you
realise how powerful it is when you accept it as a defining part of your
journey.

So writing has been my oldest friend through thick and thin. She always
keeps my secrets to herself. She never judged me or made me feel like
I should be anyone other than myself. She was always there when I
needed her. Not only was she my oldest friend, but probably one of my
first friends that I could truly be honest and myself with.

Before I could be honest and share my truth with anyone else, I first had to be willing to share it with myself.

When I spend time in nature, for me it feels like meditation. Although I also use meditation as a tool it is not something I learnt how to benefit from right away. Our relationship was a slow burn. It took me a few years along with persistence and some support, to help me see how amazing it is.

There is some research that talks about the chemistry and vibration of the planet, and how the sounds of nature and animals support us in getting back into rhythm with Mother Earth. As much as I love the science behind it all, for me what I love most is how it makes me feel. Being in nature is one of those few times that my mind is still. When I don't feel the need to have to do, and do and do. Even being at the beach! It's one of the few times we can lay down and not do anything and not actually call ourselves "lazy". How ridiculous is that, that we have confused relaxing, with laziness?!

Being with nature reminds me about just how small I am and the problems I think I have. When I sit under a tree, or I am looking out into the ocean or a lake, the mountains or up at the stars… I am reminded that I am not alone. I gain some perspective and it gives me the space to get to the core of what I am feeling and why I am feeling that way. It is an easy way for me to calm my mind, feel expansive and remember that all is well in the world.

Meditation, whether in silence or with some form of audio stimulation, has supported me greatly in releasing feelings particularly anger, sadness, forgiveness and tapping back into gratitude and love. When I am angry or upset, often the last thing I want to do is talk to anyone. So one of the best ways I have found to understand myself, and release some of that residual anger is to release it in a healthy way that doesn't hurt anyone in the process. Lighting a candle while I write and sometimes burning a letter has also been a tool I have used many many times. This way I can be 150% honest without having to worry about how my feelings will be received, if it will hurt someone and questioning if I am being selfish. When I am releasing, it is purely just for me and eventually becomes love I want to give. I am often also visualising giving my troubles and pain to Mother Nature for her to transmute into love.

I have gotten some of my best business ideas and solutions through meditation and calming my mind. Sitting in the silence, being with myself and getting off technology. Sometimes we can get so stressed about a situation but when we are able to step away from it, we realise the solution was right under our noses, we just needed to look at it with a different perspective.

Speaking to someone you love and trust. The very first person I shared my personal story to was a couple of my best friends who didn't happen to know each other. It was too difficult to hide it from my best friends and it was inevitably going to come up in conversation when it was all that I was thinking about!

Here is my checklist when sharing something super personal and intimate with someone, especially if this is the first time sharing it with anyone other than myself. It is important to be discerning with the first few people you share yourself with because how they respond can either encourage or discourage you from opening up your heart and being vulnerable.

So how do we know who to best share ourselves with?

- ☐ Do you trust them 100%?
- ☐ Do you trust that they won't put you down?
- ☐ Do you know that they love you unconditionally and have your best interest at heart?
- ☐ Does it feel safe to tell them? Can they truly listen and hold space for you without wanting to change the subject out of uncomfortableness?
- ☐ Do you trust that they won't judge or shame you?

If all of these boxes are ticked, it's pretty safe to say they are a great person to share your feelings with.

*Be specific about who's opinion of you matters. Feedback you should listen to should come from **people who love you, not DESPITE your imperfections but BECAUSE of your imperfections and vulnerability.***
~ Brené Brown

Hiring a coach/mentor/guide you trust and resonate with who is further along the path than you. Hiring someone with the purpose of your transformation means that it is going to be highly uncomfortable and often triggering. Especially working one-on-one with a person because it is a very intimate relationship. There is nowhere to run or hide. I have found this to be true, not only with working with my many mentors but also when working with my own clients. People who have one-on-one support usually get more transformation and more results simply because a mentor or guide can see where your blind spots are before you do. They can see the challenges before you know there is one there. They know the solution before you need it. The feedback loop with a mentor or a guide is much faster than any other support available.

This is the reason why I have trained and hired other coaches to support in the delivery of my signature program *Conscious Coaching 101* – I want to support as many people as possible in being able to get paid in sharing their gifts, story and experience in a heart-centre, integrity driven way. I am very clear I cannot work with every single person one-on-one.

If you are someone who has already exercised a strong muscle in being brutally honest with yourself, facing the truth, getting feedback and making changes without feeling bad or thinking there is something wrong with you, you could likely be ready for that next level of support and feedback. It may be in improving your life, health, relationships or business. Whatever area of your life that you are wanting to reach a new level in, it's going to mean letting new information in. A new perspective. Ideally from someone who has already walked that path. If you would like some guidance and the checklist I and my clients use to choose the right mentor for you please head to www.TheNakedYouBook.com/Resources to claim your free gift.

If you want to know more about The *Conscious Coaching 101* program, any of our other programs, or you are looking for a specific kind of coach from health to life, to spirituality, business and sales, connect with us at www.TheNakedYouBook.com/Resources

With ALL of these methods, it is normal for there to be tears and laughter. This is inevitable when we are honest with ourselves and on the journey of healing. I notice that for me when I am holding back tears, it is often because I don't want to acknowledge how I am feeling. It has been years of practise for me to allow myself to cry. In front of an audience that I am speaking to, a client, on a podcast or video interview, with a friend, family member, my daughter or stranger.

We know that disease is just dis-ease in the body. We must release our emotions. Emotions are just energy in motion. We must allow them to move through us. When we stop the energy, we stop the flow.

When we stop the flow, we stop feeling like ourselves and we start feeling like life is working against us. But what if it is us that is working against life?

~ Journal on the questions below ~

QUESTIONS
- How can I be more honest with myself?
- Which of these four areas (journaling, nature/meditation, speaking to someone, hiring support) will be the one which supports me the most with where I am in life at the moment?
- When can I make time for myself?
- When can I schedule it in my calendar to ensure this happens?

If you're brave with your life, if you choose to live in the arena, you're going to get your ass kicked! You're going to fall, you're going to fail, you're going to know heartbreak. It's a choice I make every day. Today I choose courage over comfort…
If you are going to be brave, you are GOING to fail!
~ Brené Brown

Are you willing to fail?

What's your relationship to failing? To being less than perfect? To getting things wrong? Can you keep moving forward when it's hard, when you are being asked to dig deep? When you are getting to see what you are made of. When you are being tested. Are you willing to get it wrong? Are you able to trust yourself more than your fear or insecurities? Can you have faith that you are being divinely guided and supported?

Not just are you willing, but are you taking action? The action necessary to move you in the right direction? The direction that you choose.

I coach people all over the world in building their business from scratch (literally not receiving a dollar yet) to making a six-figure income, and the number one thing that stops people from not making money doing what they love is a lack of action. Why is there a lack of action? Most people are so scared to get it wrong. Most people aren't willing to do anything until they know they can do it perfectly and get the perfect result. Of course this makes sense if they don't have a proven strategy or any feedback (from a coach or a mentor). A reality that hit me personally was that…

I can no longer be in the illusion of what's possible, if I do it and fail. I cannot imagine myself having this super-successful book when it's not successful when it launches.

How ridiculous is that! As I write it, I can see just how silly that sounds. Firstly, the success of this book doesn't define me, my value and my worth. Secondly, of course I can still hope and imagine the book is and will be successful. And thirdly, just writing the book to me is a success and an accomplishment. But just because I know this innately it doesn't mean that the fear doesn't still creep in or that I was never paralysed in overwhelm. I just learnt how to get back up faster. I just learnt that it doesn't define me. I just learned that no matter what I just have to keep moving forward. Even when it's painful. Especially… when it's painful!! Getting up can mean just getting out of bed one day, smiling another day, writing on another day, and learning to love and forgive on another day. Obstacles, failures and setbacks are inevitable! Are you willing to persist and grow through it?

I truly believe that the reason why it is so hard to be a full-time entrepreneur is because we are tested in every possible way to see if we are willing to keep on keeping on when it gets tough. Because eventually when it gets "too hard" only something truly worth fighting for is what will pull us to keep going. And often we realise it's not about us. The famous quote says we are more willing to do more for others than we are willing to do for ourselves. I have had to dig deeper and deeper every time I hit a new challenge in my business. It has only made me stronger!

If you choose to be an entrepreneur, it's going to be challenging... It's designed that way to filter out those who are committed to making an impact. The difference in mindset is are you willing to train yourself to look for a solution or will you allow yourself to get consumed by doubt and fear?

Brené Brown speaks of this inner critic as our gremlins! Have you built the self-awareness to notice when it is your gremlins? Or have you allowed yourself to be so consumed to think that you are every thought you have ever had? Do you have the courage to feel the depths of your pain, perceived failure and the anticipation of your fears at the same time not allowing it to control you?

I heard Denzel Washington say something that for me perfectly summarises why I chose to be an entrepreneur. Denzel said:

No matter what, life is going to be hard. Whether you do follow your dreams or you don't. If you don't follow your dreams, life is easy at the beginning and hard at the end. When you follow your dreams life is hard at the beginning and easy at the end. So it's not about choosing what is easy or hard, but about choosing which hard you will experience?

Most people won't do what they think is too hard. Most people search for immediate gratification over long term gain. It's not about choosing what's easy or hard, but are you willing to go through the hard times now, for an easier future?

> *Failure is not the opposite of success, it is a part of it.*
> ~ Arianna Huffington

~ Listen to *Brave* by Sara Bareilles ~

~ Take a moment here to stop, reflect and journal on anything that has resonated, taught or inspired you ~

> *Feeling is awareness.*
> ~ Scott Oldford

When I interviewed my amazing mentor Scott Oldford for this book, we spoke in detail about alignment. Something we agreed on, is that in order to have alignment, we must first have self-awareness. If you want to watch or listen to the full interview, go to www.TheNakedYouBook.com/Resources

Think back to a movie that actually rips your heart open. Ones that come to my mind are *The Notebook* and *A Star is Born* with Lady Gaga. It almost feels excruciating to feel that pain and to witness those journeys…

But at the same time I also notice a depth of love that I realise is either absent or present in my life. When I was single, it reminds me it is better to have loved and lost than to have not loved at all. Since being with my loving partner, I cry in gratitude for my family.

So in a way I learn to love the pain! Ladies, how many of us intentionally put on a sad break up or love song when we have just broken up with our partner. It's like we CHOOSE to be in pain!

What if the secret to being fully present in our life is to embrace the full spectrum of emotions? What if pain and pleasure are just two sides of the same coin? What if we did not run away from all of our emotions of pain or pleasure?

When I think back on journeying with plant medicine in the jungle, it is honestly one of the scariest, confronting, hardest things I have ever done. But at the same time, one of the most beautiful, heart opening, loving and present experiences I have ever had. I could not have one experience without the other. I could not feel the depth of the love I have for humanity and every living thing, if I didn't first come to the realisation of how much pain I was in on behalf of my fellow man.

I had spent many years of my life running from the pain. Running from myself. Running from my truth… But I found that I became increasingly unhappy… Years later I heard a quote from Brené Brown which made so much sense to me.

We cannot selectively numb

I wondered why I wasn't happy. Why I couldn't feel joy and deep love. Because without realising, I also numbed the joy!

A big part of embracing all of who I am means, when I feel like crying, I will allow myself to cry. As women we apologise for getting upset, for crying, for not being what is expected of us! "F*** that", is what I say to that. I will cry to my partner, to my friends, in a cafe, at a restaurant, with a client, when I am being interviewed or whenever I want to.

I have reframed and shifted my perception of what it means to be in pain. What it means to be heart-broken. What it means to have your world shatter. It doesn't mean that it's easy, but every time I allow my heart to break, I can quieten down enough to sense more love coming into my life. More presence. More gratitude. Gratitude for the moments when I am NOT in pain. Like those 30 seconds between contractions going through labour. They felt like heaven! Haha

> ~ Journal on the questions below ~

QUESTIONS
- What emotions am I running away from?
- On a scale of 1-10 how much time and space am I giving myself to be able to really listen and hear my own feelings and what is true for me?
- How can I embrace more of my emotions? This could be journaling more or expressing your emotions to those whom you feel it is safe to do so.

Your insecurities are not a reason, to not show up and serve
~ Nina Concepcion

A lot of people stop aiming and stop having goals when they realise they feel undeserving or unworthy. Most of us feel undeserving or unworthy at some point especially at the start of any new journey. The majority of us have not been brought up with conscious parents that know when what they are saying and teaching – although it comes from love, is hindering our personal growth and confidence. How much we believe we deserve is something we can CONTINUALLY work on. It is also not an excuse to not show up or keep going.

People who have a strong sense of love and belonging, simply believe they are worth of love and belonging.
~ Brené Brown

You cannot just switch off what is calling you from within.

Often we fool ourselves into thinking what it is we want based on logic. That we can just turn off wanting to make an impact. I tried this! It kept calling me back time and time again.

In reality, what we go after, what we move towards and attract, is based on what we feel we deserve. When I think about the life I am creating now, I wonder, what stopped me in creating this sooner? I didn't truly believe I had the capacity, ability and skill to be able to do what I do now. I used to say to myself *you're not good enough to do that. Who are you to think you can do that!? You're nobody.* The funny thing is, if someone had told me I was doing what I am doing now, although I believed it was possible deep down, my dreams and visions were covered with fear and doubt.

Now looking back…

I believe the secret is in action.

"Action Precedes Confidence"
~ Nina Concepcion

If I did not first put myself out there, I would not KNOW what I was capable of.

We are stronger than we think! But we don't realise until we are put into a situation and find ourselves handling it better than we thought we would have.

Until we see the results for ourselves, until we have the experience of doing it, it is just a belief. Simply a thought and a mental construct. But once we take action and see it become a reality, the belief becomes a fact. Which fuels our confidence in being able to achieve something. Which then gives us the confidence to start thinking or aiming for things we never thought possible.

This is when the impossible becomes potential and possible.

As a "Conscious Sales" Coach, many of my clients come to me simply because they either don't know how to make any sales in their business or they don't know how to push through that glass ceiling, unable to hit consistent $10k+ months in their business, to give them a comfortable full-time income. My clients often hit a new record month AFTER they shift their beliefs through action. A belief can be changed in an instant or over time. It's done through taking strategic clear action, the power of osmosis of being part of a supportive community of other coaches and borrowing my belief in them until their belief takes over. My clients have gone from $0 to making their first couple thousand dollars in a couple weeks… from making inconsistent average $5k months to their first $50k month! What do they all have in common?

My Conscious Sales Method is proven to work time and time again globally. It is heavily dependent on the belief of our community holding the belief for each other, along with strategic action.

One example of a belief a mentor held for me was with my very first spiritual business mentor Jeffrey Slayter. He predicted that I would work with women. At the time I did not have one female client and all my clients were men!

One of the things Jeff taught me is to be discerning about everything, including what my mentors tell me. Ultimately I need to trust myself. Funnily enough though, I started attracting female clients. I didn't even TRY to! It's not like I actively went out and started going to women's circles! It's just sort of happened.

Six years later, 95% of my clients are women! I still work with some men, however most of my clients are women.

It's not that back then I didn't want to work with women, it was that I didn't BELIEVE women would want to work with me. That's why I never considered offering or working with women until that point. I didn't think other women liked me. I was bullied growing up and I didn't resonate with many girls who bitched and complained all the time about other people. Most of my friends growing up were men… well boys, because I found there was less drama in those conversations and relationships. This was my reality until I started to attract more heart-centred women who reflected back my own beliefs that I had worked hard to move through within myself. Rather than comparing ourselves with other women, we choose to lift other women up and empower each other through collaboration instead of competition. We currently have on average one referral a month that takes place within the community of amazing women (and some men) that I have created in my coaching container. This includes referring clients to other women, my clients paying to work with my other clients, my clients referring me work and vice versa.

When I thought about the type of women I wanted to work with back six years ago, rather than coming from a place of abundance and love, I was coming from a place of fear and insecurity. Luckily though, I still took action and listened to what the universe was putting in front of me. When a friend was having trouble landing her first ever paying coaching clients (when she had done every course under the sun), I couldn't help but share with her that I could help her. She was the seed that was planted with what I was capable of. If I hadn't offered to help someone in need, I may not be doing the work I am doing now in my business.

Do you have the courage to dream big?

Life is not what people say it is. It is what you make of it. It is what you CHOOSE for it to be and what you consistently take action upon. It is what you BELIEVE it to be. And you have the power to choose and believe differently.

Unless you're willing to move THROUGH
the immediacy of feeling uncomfortable,
you will continue to be pulled back into your comfort zone,
what's known, and predictable.
The truth is that we need to get UNCOMFORTABLE enough to make a
change. Unless our current reality is more painful than doing nothing,
nothing will change because we will continue to do nothing about it.
~Nina Concepcion

Not making a decision at all is in truth, a lie we tell ourselves to justify not taking action.

If I just ignore my unhappy relationship it will just eventually get better – does it!?

If I just ignore the fact that I'm gaining more and more weight from overeating – do you get to lose weight by not doing anything about it?

I'm just going to ignore that I hate my job and I'll just get used to it one day – do you?

So either you create that internal shift. Or something outside of you will force you to make a decision.

Do you have the courage to take radical self-responsibility?

Complaining seems to be the option for most people above really wanting to live a different life. People say that they want change. But they're unwilling to do anything about it.

Do you have the courage to get really honest about what you truly want? Or will you just continue to complain?

Most people say they want a successful business. They say they want to make a full-time income. They say they want to inspire others.

But most people are unwilling to invest into themselves. Most people are unwilling to ask for help and support. Most people think they can make a legacy all on their own. Most people are UNWILLING to leave their comfort zone. Most people are unwilling to stretch and move past overwhelm to learn a new skill required to get their business to the next level. Most people are unwilling to share their true feelings in fear of getting hurt.

There is a reason that currently in my industry, only 1% of coaches reach a six-figure income in their business.

One huge reason that stops people from even getting ahead is their unwillingness to look at the reality of their situation and ask for help.

Ask for help… Not because you're weak…
But to remain strong.
~ Les Brown.

If you do not have the courage to be wrong, to be told you're wrong, to take responsibility and make changes….

Nothing is going to change.

Your results won't change.

Your life won't change.

This truly hit me as a young 20-year-old in real estate. I was a proud, ego-driven young woman. Just like my dad, I despised being wrong! Apparently… I always had to have the last word! Haha

My boss said

Nina I'd rather be wrong and rich… than right and miserable. People who think they're right all the time never learn and don't see their

mistakes. Those who are always willing to learn… improve and grow…! Which one do you want to be?

I then made the decision, from then on, I am willing to be wrong.

~ Journal on the questions below ~

QUESTIONS
- Do you have the courage to believe another version of your life is possible?
- Do you have the courage to believe you are bigger than your circumstances?
- Do you have the courage to believe there is another version of you that you can step into instantly if you choose?
- Do you have the courage to think for yourself?
- Do you have the courage to believe in your ability to figure anything out?
- Do you have the courage to believe in yourself?
- Do you have the courage to be seen and heard for all of who you are?
- Do you have the courage to be you?

CHAPTER 5

Space & Stillness

CHAPTER 5

Space &
Stillness

*Almost all of life's greatest works of art, music, literature, and drama
have emerged out of the genius of melancholy, or out of human beings
who have allowed melancholy a deep place in their inner lives.*
~ Richard Rudd *(The Gene Keys)*

Life is going to have its ups and downs. Peaks and valleys. But when we have people who we surround ourselves with who remind us who we are, how amazing we are, and how loved we are… then regardless of if we are going through a high or a low in life, it's worthwhile because we have loved ones to share the journey with.

Have you ever given yourself enough space to notice?

In the midst of one of the most challenging things you've ever experienced, you can find bliss, joy and space in between the moments of agony.

There is a void that becomes so undeniably apparent when we are alone. This doesn't necessarily mean lonely. Or isolated.

But rather the opposite.

When you give yourself more space FOR yourself than you've had in a while, subtle energies have the opportunity to come into the light and the forefront of your awareness.

Pain doesn't have to be painful. It can just be a different feeling, a sensation. A different way of being. All you have to do is observe it without judgment.

I remember when my ex-boyfriend (whom I lost my virginity to) told me he wasn't in love with me anymore, I was absolutely beside myself. But I decided to still go and do something for me that same day. It was my first time snorkelling by myself. I was in New Caledonia. To my surprise, I found peace, understanding and acceptance through being in the ocean. By being in a different world, it gave me perspective. I remembered it wasn't all about me and what I wanted.

I remember when I had confronted the other person involved in that TPE… I was absolutely s**ting myself counting down the hours and minutes until that meeting. But I took in some deep breaths and found the strength to love myself in a way I didn't know I was capable of. I allowed myself to stop looking outside of me and go within to find space and love.

I remember when my partner and I broke up for a week, even through the pain I felt a love for myself and him that I wouldn't have uncovered if we didn't take that break.

I remember telling myself that the heartbreak reminds me that I'm alive. It reminds me that I care. It reminds me that I'm open. It reminds me that I am human.

For so long I lived numbing my feelings. I didn't realise what I was doing to myself. I literally spent years trying to protect myself.

When I was in real estate my boss asked me a question about my ex that changed how I look at everything in life. He asked me *where in your life are you holding yourself back? It's affecting your ability to grow.* He just sat there waiting for an answer after I kept denying there was anything holding me back (I truly believed I wasn't!) My response was *IF…. there WAS anything I guess it would be being single. But I choose to be and I have forgiven my ex.*

Are you ready for the question that changed my life…?

He asked me

Have you forgiven yourself?

The stream of tears was instant! It hadn't occurred to me that I blamed myself!

That night I called my ex with the intention of not having my walls up, getting closure and to express how much our break up really hurt me. Because up until that point, I was too proud to ever let him see that I was hurt. That is what I thought being strong was – pretending not to feel. I finally discovered that holding onto pain doesn't hurt anyone but me. *Hurt people, hurt people.* We unconsciously want to hurt others when we are hurt. I didn't want to hurt him (or get payback) or hurt myself anymore… I was done playing the blame game.

When you think of your life, when you're in pain, when you are hurting…. How can you breathe through the overwhelm? How can you heal it from the inside instead of projecting your hurt onto others?

There were times that I couldn't even think of taking each day by day. Each moment in itself felt like too much. How can you take each moment one moment at a time?

Yes, it's going to feel like a lot! It's going to feel hard. It's going to feel like you are stretching. But the difference between feeling overwhelmed and stretching while we grow is a matter of mindset.

Will you choose to have the courage to keep moving forward?

Will you allow it to be too hard? Or will you see this circumstance as an opportunity to grow into the next version of yourself. That this situation is just training you to become a more evolved version of yourself.

Firstly learn how to hold space for yourself, how can you express it healthily through a means that doesn't include anyone being affected else? (Like journaling or meditating like we discussed in the last chapter). Then leaning into expressing it and sharing yourself with those you love and trust, and finally if you choose to, sharing your message with others, like sharing your story, helping others or turning your message into a business.

Free Humanity

There's nothing or no one there
at times we feel alone
but really Mother Earth, has got us
even if to us it's unknown

our eyes may not be open
we may think our hearts have been impure
our arms may not be spread apart
to the point that we feel obscure

we hide the truth and seek hiding
from what really is
that she has us
every moment, every breeze is a kiss

there's healing in the rain
there's love beneath us in the ground
when are we going to choose to stop
and actually listen to the sound

when we feel alone
she's always right there beside you
she's right there beside me
even when you don't her want to

when you are willing to feel
and just get out of your mind
you'll get out of your way
all of a sudden you won't be so blind

take in the meaning
with what you feel in your heart
accept the love around you
you will never really be a PART

you are everything
at the same time not at all
you are enormous
at the same time incredibly small

it's liberating to accept and feel
that this is your essence, your being
it's not always and even often
what you think you're seeing

~ Nina Concepcion

For the Entrepreneur…

With my clients I am always telling them that we often cannot hold space for someone and guide them through something that we have not been able to go through ourselves. This is because if we are not able to be with the depth of our own pain, we will unconsciously run away from it when others are facing their own pain. But when we learn to hold and love ourselves as we break open, the more we are able to energetically hold that for others as well.

I am seeing this unfold more and more… as I grow my business. As I grow as a person… as I grow my wealth. For those of you who feel and hear the whispers to birth a business, book, idea into the world….

Your business is really just the ultimate test to your commitment to humanity.

If it was easy – everyone would be doing it. If you TRULY believe in making a change, you will stick through it when it is hard. Like ANY relationship, it doesn't mean you won't want to give up or take a break… but it means you continue to work at it. [1]

I feel like every obstacle, challenge and heartbreak I have been through, has shaped my experience, skills and strength to be able to serve at the degree I do. Which means that in order for me to serve and impact more people, there will be more pain and challenges to move through.

I used to think in terms of what I wanted… But now that I am able to take care of myself and my family… my attention has diverted more so to how can I make the biggest impact? It is less about me and more about the ripples I am co-creating.

What else is adamantly clear is that we cannot pour from an empty cup. Nor do we pour the same when we pour from a half full cup compared to an overflowing cup.

I serve at my best when I am overflowing!!!

It has been a constant unlearning for me… Letting go of the guilt of putting myself first. From a logical standpoint, the truth is I don't even need much!

I was joking around with a good friend the other day and we were saying how we have invested literally $00k+ plus in mentors and coaches in the last 18 months alone and yet we feel guilty for spending $100 in buying something for ourselves.

This is conditioning at its best. Especially for women.

Give give give!!! But don't take!!

Be ok to overgive but don't accept what is too much!

How ridiculous is that!?

The lore of the universe states that for every giver there is a receiver. When we reject the gifts life gives us, we not only declare we are unworthy and to stop giving to us, but we also rob the other person of the gift and joy of giving.

So next time someone pays you a compliment, gives their time, their love, a meal, a loan or a gift... rather than feeling guilty and saying *no I can't accept this...* practice being grateful, feeling worthy, and loved and saying *thank you.*

When we are overflowing we also come from a place of abundance instead of scarcity. One way we can do this as entrepreneurs and business owners is to give gratitude through our money. Giving a commission or a referral fee is something I love to do. It stuck with me when Brendon Burchard said *50% of something is more than 100% of nothing.* Giving a commission is showing our gratitude through action, not just words.

~ Journal on the questions below ~

QUESTIONS

- How can we honour ourselves more?
- How can we honour each other more?

Stay Completed

Does anyone see these colours
does anyone feel this pain
has anyone been to this place
or am I just going insane?

does anyone understand me
or am I all alone
am I willing to confront this
and jump into the unknown

this feeling of isolation
like no one understands
feels like I'm losing myself
when I just want to expand

growth hurts too
sometimes that, I forget
but this too, I must embrace
it's ok to get upset

I just need someone to be here
to tell me I'll be ok
to hold me and comfort me
knowing we'll find a way

these fears I'm facing on my own
are surfacing through my being
it hurts, I'm bleeding
but it's the only way of seeing

it's the only way to really heal
to accept how it is I'm feeling
I must not resist it
even if I may be screaming

like waves washing over me
the peace will come
just be patient and have faith
it'll come like the sun

so just hang in there
things will get better again soon
the universe has got you
you just need to get back in tune

be one with the music
not just the circumstance you're in
yes you're in this physical form
but you are one from within

stay with yourself
and stay committed
stay in your heart
and stay completed

The Power Of Vulnerability

The Power Of Vulnerability

*Connection is what gives purpose and meaning to our lives. Connection as a result of **authenticity**. The whole-hearted are willing to let go of who they thought they should be, in order to be who they were, which is needed for connection…*
Vulnerability is not weakness. Vulnerability is our most accurate measurement of courage.
~ Brené Brown

It all starts with vulnerability. Without vulnerability there is no connection! The amazing Dr Brené Brown, the renowned researcher on shame and vulnerability says, *"Vulnerability is the birth place of love, belonging, joy, courage and empathy, along with creativity, innovation and change."* Just pay attention to the people you feel closest to. Don't you feel they truly know you at a level that others don't? Perhaps because you don't let others see certain sides of you. Or maybe it simply just doesn't feel safe to share all of yourself with many or most people.

Once you know how to hold that space for yourself and you are steady in your own emotions, power and level of security, it doesn't actually matter what anyone says about you or to you. It doesn't affect you. What I mean by it won't affect you, is that you will be OKAY and you KNOW deep down that you will be ok with whatever happens. Because at the end of the day YOU have got YOUR BACK. And really, you are the only person who is going to be spending 24/7 for the rest of your life with you, so your perception of yourself… is what matters more than anyone else's.

My journey with vulnerability has not been an easy one. While I share probably THE most vulnerable story I have, I encourage you again to bring some awareness to how you are feeling, what memories come up for you while I share. I have gotten some of my biggest insights into myself and my life through listening to other people's stories.

I was about 12 years old when I first confronted 'him' about the TPE. This was the first time in my life I had to grow up and put my big girl panties on. No one was going to save me at that moment. It was up to me to make a decision if I wanted to not feel like I hated my life anymore. Yes of course it was incredibly hard, challenging, scary, astonishingly painful, especially at such a young age.

I remember it so vividly still to this day… I think I cried and cried and cried until I was all cried out. Until I sat there in stillness, numbness, looking out into the distance. Bracing myself. My mum offered to take me away, but I said no. A clear and unequivocal – No. I had to do this. I had to confront him. Him and my younger cousins were already on their way there. I had to be there for them. It was the first time my dad had ever told me he loved me. It was a life-changing moment on many levels!

I remember saying to myself. Be strong. This is a moment you'll probably never get a chance to do ever again. Stay strong. Be the voice for your two younger cousins. Although he didn't admit what he did… I felt relieved… I felt I could finally start moving forward. I feel like I was letting go of the anxiety and fear that had built up.

So many tears had been shed. I can't even count how many times my heart has broken for that little girl.

She just wanted someone to protect her.
She just wanted someone to take her away.

But in the end she had to have the courage and strength to save herself.

Are you stepping up or waiting for someone to come save you?

You can see how easy it would be to hate the world. To never let a man touch me. To never want to be intimate. To want to keep everyone at arms' length to avoid being hurt. To stay angry especially when the person denied what he did to my cousins and myself…

This was the easy way out.

The truth is I still kept a very thick armour up for a while…

After about a year into deciding to leave real estate, I decided to sell my home and move to Bali. I was getting further into debt not being able to pay my mortgage as a struggling entrepreneur, and I wanted to go on an adventure and live abroad. But before I left, I wanted to tie up any loose ends in Australia. There was one main demon that came to mind. That TPE.

I have forgiven him… but have I truly forgiven him? Am I healed? How will I know I have healed from it? Nina… if you are going to make the difference you know you are here to make, you need to do this. I will know I am healed because I can see him and not feel like I hate him. I will know I have forgiven him when I can have love for him, SIMPLY because he's a human being and we are all deserving of love.

I once again braced myself for another meeting (or confrontation).

The conversation with my boss mentioned in the last chapter really planted a seed for me. I truly started to realise that the only person I was just hurting by keeping people at arms' length, was myself. This is the mindset that was the catalyst to me choosing to live my life vulnerably. This second confrontation was just another affirmation that there is no other way to live my life or run my business.

My intention for this meeting was to get closure and to also give him the opportunity to apologise. Although I was not expecting or attached to receiving an apology. I wanted to forgive him, even without an apology from him. Even if I think he did or didn't deserve it, I wanted to forgive him, for me.

The difference between the both confrontations, other than my intention, is that THIS time I was willing to be vulnerable and show my emotions. I wasn't going to pretend anything. Rather than feeling like I needed to defend or protect myself, I just held myself in a bubble of love, trusting that I would be ok. Externally – it was also a public cafe so I knew I was safe. I wanted to go into this interaction with my heart open, ready and willing to listen and forgive.

This second meeting was by far one of the most powerful experiences I have ever had. A few months later, I also decided to interview him for this book because I believe it took a level of vulnerability for him to meet with me as well as me meeting with him. The below resource is a combination of what happened during those interactions as well as the interview discussing our meetings. If you would like a written copy of that interview, please head to www.TheNakedYouBook.com/Resources.

Here is what happened…

After almost two decades he finally apologised. He admitted what he did for the first time in his life and he shared that for a while he thought it was normal – the same thing had happened to him! It wasn't until after I confronted him the first time, that he really stopped to think of how wrong it was.

I asked him *What were you thinking when I asked you to meet with me this time around?*

To be honest, it was the first time I have ever been excited to say sorry to anyone. I was f***ing scared but more excited to say sorry. I didn't care if you swore at me, yelled at me, or hit me… All I knew is I just wanted to say sorry because I have wanted to say sorry for ages.

He fell into depression due to what had happened and it's taken a long time for him to forgive himself.

I know it was that meeting. Ever since then I just know I've been happier... I felt like a massive weight had been lifted off my shoulders. I was literally able to sleep a lot better after that meeting with you...

The biggest thing I have learnt about myself is that I am able to forgive a lot more. Because if you and I are able to forgive me for what I've done, I should be able to forgive others for what they've done too.

I also asked him about guilt. *Is there a part of you that holds onto that guilt with my other cousins because you may never end up getting their forgiveness?*

*Yeah definitely. Even though I feel I'm healed as well, I still feel that heavy weight with what I did to them as well. As I said to you, I feel there was a weight that was lifted off my shoulders when you forgave me, but it's still heavy. It's just lighter because **I feel your forgiveness has helped me heal.** There is still going to be that weight of regret of not being able to say sorry to them....*

When you first confronted me, I denied it, but I was deeply sorry. I didn't know how to apologise, or how to approach you. I didn't apologise out of fear of you not accepting my apology and not wanting to talk to me. I wasn't sure if you guys would understand me or forgive me.

<blockquote>
Shame is the fear of disconnection.
Is there something about me that if other people know it or see it,
I won't be worthy of connection.
The – I am not... blank enough.
In order for connection to happen we have to allow ourselves to be seen.
~ Brené Brown
</blockquote>

This experience has really shown me the… **power of forgiveness!**

After meeting with him for a couple hours, I sat in the car talking on the phone with one of my best friends. She said to me *Nina, do you realise the healing you have given him? Healing that only YOU could have given him? It's ironic that you are the one who was "abused" and yet you have helped him heal.* It hit me just how powerful that experience was. I sat there crying in gratitude, feeling lighter than I had in years!

I was finally coming back to love.

From then on I made a conscious decision for the rest of my life to BE vulnerable… because my default reaction is to NOT be vulnerable. The alternative would mean the rest of my life feeling alone, misunderstood, disconnected and unhappy. This is NOT something I desired. I wanted all the opposite things. Connection, love, belonging, joy, happiness and to really just forget and not think about having to protect myself every single day!

Being naked on the front cover of this book is a metaphor for vulnerability. To remind me that being vulnerable IS scary, but in order to live the quality of life I desire, it is not a choice anymore. It's a non-negotiable. It MUST be done. Now, for me, choosing to be vulnerable is a lifestyle choice. We think vulnerability opens us up for rejection, but not choosing to be vulnerable and not having connection is actually the ultimate rejection – self-rejection. What a safe way to protect yourself from being loved if you never allow anyone to love you.

The whole-hearted believe what made them vulnerable
is what made them beautiful.
Vulnerability isn't comfortable or excruciating but necessary
~ Brené Brown

I can honestly say that if I continued to stay guarded and not let people in, I would DEFINITELY not be where I am today, doing what I do, living the life I have, with the people I love. I feel connected, I feel like I belong and I feel like I can be me! Not to mention I barely think about that experience anymore unless I am sharing my story. I have learnt to love parts of me that I never thought was possible, including my most wounded part of me, this part of me.

> ~ Journal on the questions below ~

QUESTIONS
- What are some of the experiences and stories that have happened to me that I am most scared to share?
- How can I more easily open up to those I trust?
- What do I intuitively and emotionally feel I would be missing out on if I don't let people see the real me? What would this mean for the quality of life and relationships I desire?

"We can never truly feel the depth of loving another person and being loved by them, if we don't first allow ourselves to be vulnerable and to really be seen."
~ Nina Concepcion

For the Entrepreneur…

As a service provider and entrepreneur, we must understand that the average consumer is reluctant, sceptical and cautious. So it is us to lead. It is us that most first open up our hearts. It is the US that must be vulnerable first. If we can lead and show them that there is nothing to fear, and that we are not scared of getting hurt, we show them through action, that they too can trust that they are safe and that they are held.

This is the first step and the premise to "Conscious Sales".

~ Listen to *Roar* by Katy Perry ~

CHAPTER 7

Values

CHAPTER 7

Values

Those who stand for nothing, fall for everything.
~ Alexander Hamilton

What do you stand for? What do you value? What does it mean to honour yourself? When you see someone being bullied would you stand up for them? Do you stand up for them?

There are a couple ways we can look at values. The first way is the traditional sense of principles or standard of behaviour. We must first need to be aware of what we value, who we are, who we are not.

I am going to toss a few words around to get you started. As you read these words, write down what most resonates with you and any other thoughts or values you think of.

Honesty, love, vulnerability, fun, quality of value, quality, honour, transparency, loyalty, respect, compassion, kindness, forgiveness, integrity, empowerment, authenticity, courage, faith, service, duty, peace, hope, gratitude, growth.

Often we don't know what we value until we are put in a situation that forces us to decide.

When I was in real estate, I had countless opportunities daily to lie, manipulate and take advantage of people. At first I could feel the pressure of having to be like others I saw – the majority of society… But when I felt what was right for me, it was very clear to me that I would rather not make any sales and conduct business ethically as opposed to being successful, but feeling like a fraud. This is obviously easier said than done. Once the pressure started to compound with my lack of results, I questioned if I was cut out for real estate. The more I said no to what was against my values, the easier it was to keep saying no. The pressure internally of what felt right for me was no longer there because I was clear with what I was and wasn't willing to do. Because I was not willing to compromise, it made me question if this is where I truly belonged if I was expected to be a certain way.

Fortunately my boss in real estate, who was also my first mentor, did not put pressure on me like I thought he would have.

He allowed me to honour my own values whilst I built my skill level. My values of integrity, honesty and transparency is not what determines the success of every real estate agent. I know plenty of sleazy successful real estate agents. However, it would be what determined MY success in my career and my life. People expected me to lie and tell them what they wanted to hear. So when I took the time to really be honest with them and go out of my way to find the correct answer, I built trust with my clients that went beyond the 12 week transaction.

In real estate there is something called the golden chain of referrals. It normally takes about five to ten years for this to happen. My golden chain of referrals started to happen within my first year. They became loyal to me. Simply because I honoured my values. I got to be me. I didn't have to fit into this mould of what I thought was set in stone. I could pave a new path for myself in an already existing system that worked.

I had to find and discover those lines. The boundaries of my job but still being me. How can I close this deal without sacrificing my values? How can I answer this client's questions without lying? How can I be honest without jeopardising the sale? This was MY point of difference.

In life we are constantly given opportunities to discover what matters to us, what our boundaries are, what we are and aren't willing to give of ourselves. I was willing to give my time, energy, focus and undivided attention. I was not willing to give up my values.

The thing is if we never leave our house and never take any action or experience anything how do we ever learn? We simply need to move through the fear. The most important piece in doing this is mindset.

In real estate, I never once had a door slammed in my face. I have never once been yelled at or been accused of being sleazy or manipulative. Challenge yourself to see if you can find the answer below when I share how clients described working with me.

"Nina made the process simple and easy. She genuinely cared and was always there when we needed anything."

The late Wayne Dyer said:

When you change the way you look at things, the things you look at change.

I deconstructed who I want to be, what I would be proud of doing, and how I wanted to feel and be known for. From there I worked out my values, did those small consistent steps daily and ta da! We live a life achieving our goal through honouring our values. We really do create our reality and it all starts from mindset. A shift in our thoughts and beliefs creates the shift in our actions and results.

If you are someone who wants to shift your disempowering mindset around sales, learn how to come from a heart-centred approach, and want start to move through the fear of rejection head to www. TheNakedYouBook.com/Resources

The other way we can look at values is through the lens of Dr John Demartini's teachings. I had the absolute privilege of interviewing Dr Demartini for this book. Below I share his perspective on values, authenticity and how it impacts our life and business.

Dr Demartini says that our values create our voids. He says that your values arise from and are therefore determined by your conscious or unconscious voids (what you perceive as most missing). What you perceive as most missing (void) in your life therefore becomes what you perceive as most important (value).

For example, Dr Demartini's values include travel, teaching and learning. This stems from his childhood when he was labelled dyslexic and a teacher told his parents that he would never read, write or amount to anything. So what did he do? He invested his entire life into doing just that – making a difference!

Can you think of a situation where someone told you you couldn't do anything, and after moving through the sadness, it made you stronger and more determined? Uncovering your voids is a start to uncovering your values.

> *To know thyself is the beginning of wisdom.*
> ~ Socrates

Step 1, we need to have **self-awareness**. Discover your highest values. Is it a fantasy, society, others, or truly your own values?

Step 2, to have the **courage** to *consciously* choose your values and to stick to it. Instead of unconsciously trying to be something you're not. This is also what ends up maximising self-worth and achievement. It's about doing the things daily that are highest on our values.

Optional Step 3, change your values to match your goals or choose your goals to be in alignment with your highest values. Either way, Dr Demartini say that they must be congruent in order for your life to be an authentic expression of who you are.

When we fill our days with highest value actions this is an expression of our authenticity. Congruence of our highest values and our actions is authenticity.

Authenticity is a conscious awareness of your values as well as the conscious decision to prioritise and live by it!

When I asked Dr Demartini the impact of authenticity on our life and business this was his response:

Every area of your life is impacted by authenticity. There isn't one area of your life that isn't impacted by our authenticity…

We cannot have authenticity until we can accept we are both the hero and the villain. The true authentic you, encompasses all of you! The fastest way to disempowerment is thinking you are a one-sided individual (perfection)…

We cannot find fulfilment, trying to get rid of half of who we are. At the level of our souls, there is nothing missing. We cannot see our amazement when we're addicted to a fantasy or an illusion.

What stands out for me here is the importance of self-awareness but also self-acceptance.

When you shrink yourself, you attempt to temporarily live outside your values to try and be like someone else…
Anytime you expect to live outside your own values you will self-depreciate.

We unconsciously try to be someone we are not.

We end up investing so much time trying to be something we are not. Comparing ourselves with other people's values. We fool ourselves into thinking we want that job, we want to climb that corporate ladder, we want the perfect relationship with the expensive car… because we think we need to be like others we see and admire and possibly put on a pedestal. Dr Demartini says:

I don't strive for success. I strive for fulfilment.

It is not about arriving, or about the destination. It's about the journey.

Someone else's accomplishments do not make you inadequate. Stop comparing yourself. When we think we aren't "successful" it's because

1 – We are either comparing our accomplishments with another person or people

Or

2 – We have allowed ourselves to adopt other people's values which are not ours, so we end up having invested time and energy into building a life we never really wanted in the first place.

Success is what you make it… What does success mean to you?

If what you desire for your life is a happy, healthy loving family, focus your energy on that without feeling guilty with what you spent less time on. Comparison is something that I and many of my clients have struggled with.

I heard an interview one time with Tony Robbins and Michael Jordan that stuck with me. Tony asked *Michael, why do you think you are the best basketball player of all time? What's the secret?* Michael's response was, *Most people compare themselves to me. I compare myself with the best version of myself I can be.*

Both perspectives on values I believe are empowering as there is an overlap between the two. Vulnerability is one of my values because it's been a lifelong lesson and journey of being ok to be vulnerable after I spent so many years keeping people at arm's distance, trying not to get hurt after being taken advantage of. At the same time, I am so driven to create a heart-centred community of conscious entrepreneurs because I know exactly what it's like to feel like you don't fit it or belong anywhere.

When we can get honest with our values and consciously choose our highest values, instead of unconsciously fighting for other people's values, we find true fulfilment and authenticity. This means embracing our imperfections. It means getting honest with ourselves with what we truly desire and don't desire. It means being willing to be different as opposed to sacrificing our values to fit in. It means staying in your own lane when people are on the main road.

> ~ Take some time to journal on this chapter ~

QUESTIONS
- What are your top values (behaviours and standards)?
- What are your top values (considering your voids and how you desire to live your life)?
- On a scale of 1-10 are you currently investing the majority of your day with actions that are aligned with these goals?
- How can you increase the time you invest into your highest values?
- How can you remember to stay in your own lane and stop comparing yourself to others?

If you would like to know more about values you can watch the interview with myself and Dr John Demartini and/or purchase a copy of his book *The Values Factor* go to www.TheNakedYouBook.com/Resources

CHAPTER 8

Intuition

CHAPTER 8

Intuition

I believe in intuitions and inspirations…
I sometimes FEEL that I am right.
I do not KNOW that I am.
~ Albert Einstein

Even the biggest sceptics have all had an experience of having a gut feeling. An unexplainable knowing. A feeling that something was wrong.

When my suppressed memories started to resurface I started to remember that the incident had happened a few times.

I remember after a couple times thinking, there is definitely not something right about this. There is something that is making me feel very uneasy and very uncomfortable. A feeling in the pit of my stomach that something just wasn't right.

I then made a decision to never be alone with this man ever again.

I was probably about between five and seven years old when I recall sitting on my mum's lap one night, hugging her. She asked me *Why don't you go and play?* I kept saying no. Her response was *you are going to be bored here with me. Are you sure?* I remember thinking I would much rather be bored. I stayed with my mum where I knew I was safe.

It never happened to me again… My only wish is that I had the awareness then, to also remove my younger cousins from the situation, not allowing it to happen again.

The strange thing about intuition is that if we don't follow it we often don't know what trouble we would have encountered. We often say things like *I knew I shouldn't have taken this road,* when we get stuck in traffic. But in this situation I can very clearly see the impact of what would have continued to happen if I didn't have the courage to firstly listen to my intuition and then to follow it.

This entire experience was affirmation for me, to follow my intuition when something feels adamantly clear to me that something doesn't feel right. The tricky thing with intuition is that we can have trouble distinguishing between what's fear and conditioning, compared to what our gut is trying to tell us. Here are my questions/tips for when I am questioning my intuition. The secret to answering these questions is to answer it as brutally honest as possible.

- Is one decision based out of guilt and obligation?
- Where do I feel discomfort in my body?
- Is the feeling I get more of a pull or push energy? (Intuition feels more like a pulling, like a calling.)
- Does one decision make me feel constructive and the other expansive?
- Which decision am I leaning towards and why am I leaning towards that decision?
- If I completely put my fear to the side, what decision would I make?

- What feels like the right decision to make when I put expectations and other people's opinion to the side? (Often don't make a decision based on it impacting what someone else might think or say about us e.g., people will think I am crazy.)
- Which of these decisions will I be happier with over the long term?
- Which decision will I be most proud of myself for making?
- When I think of the ideal outcome in each decision, which one feels lighter, more freeing and liberating?
- Am I tempted to do what's easy instead of what's required and necessary?
- When I calm my mind, close my eyes, breathe and let go of everything I think I should be feeling and doing, which decision is pulling me just that bit stronger at my heartstrings?
- Do I find myself saying, *I just feel like I need to do it, it feels like this is something I need to do, I just have a feeling this needs to be done*?

Intuition can also be described as your inner guidance system or the whisper of your soul.

I believe our intuition is a knowing of energy. I believe we are pulled to each moment to live a life of meaning, fulfilment and abundance. And the only way to keep living into these moments and attracting magic into your life, is to trust your intuition.

For more free tools on how to build your intuition head to www.TheNakedYouBook.com/Resources

~ Take some time to journal here ~

QUESTIONS
- What is one thing you can do to enhance and turn up the volume of your intuition so that you can't ignore it?

CHAPTER 9

Belonging & Boundaries

CHAPTER 9

Belonging & Boundaries

As I grew into my own skin as a woman, I realised and accepted that I am a no BS kind of person. Now as cool as that may sound, it means that I often trigger people! At first when people described me this way, my reaction went something like this… *Really!? Am I!?* Now, years later, I can see what they see, and now I accept it. It is natural for humans to want to be liked, loved and accepted. I have learnt to accept that not everyone will like me or what I have to say. But even now as a 31 year old writing this book, it still sometimes triggers me when someone is triggered by my "much-ness". What I do know is that…

I care more about the transformation I support my audience and clients with, over being "liked and accepted".
I care too much to not speak up about wrongdoings – even if it upsets some people.

Speaking our truth is necessary in sharing our message, and often transformation requires coming up against egos and facing our shadows. This is often triggering and uncomfortable. I know I am deeply committed to the work I do and the impact it makes in the lives of those ready, willing and open to receiving it. I wish someone had told me this reality sooner. It would have saved me years of feeling lonely, isolated and unloved.

As Brendon Burchard says *as* leaders *we need to be willing to challenge people in order to support their transformation*. But when we are choosing between saying what you know they want to hear (so that people will like you), or to speak your truth (and potentially upset people) will you choose what's easy compared to what is needed?

I have worked towards and made a conscious effort to evolve my relationships. I feel that the people in my life that I choose to surround myself with truly accept me for me. I don't need to try and be or feel like I need to be anything other than me. Now… When I am triggered, I have numerous people in my life whom I love and trust deeply to safely share my feelings with. Rather than them judging me, telling me there is something wrong with me, dismissing me or not even making time for me… the conversation goes something like this:

Nina, how can I support you, what do you need from me?
But we love this about you, if they can't accept you for you they aren't worth your time.
What do you need to do to feel better about this situation?

There is unconditional love and support whilst also taking self-responsibility. Thoughts never cross my mind anymore like *what is wrong with me, maybe I am too much for people, or maybe I am not lovable.*

I remind myself, as do my loved ones remind me, that everything I am experiencing is because

I am strong enough to handle this
This is happening for my evolution
There is a lesson to be learnt to grow into the next version of myself
If it was easy, everyone would be doing it.

I
Am
Human….

At times, I still doubt myself… I still feel insecure. At times I still feel like I am too much…

But when I have people around me that remind me of who I am when I forget, when they remind me that they love me… This is something I cannot put a price to. When my life looks like a sh**-show, this is something that continually reminds me that I am loved and that everything will be ok. Because I have people to experience life with. The highs and lows. The highs aren't any more important than the lows. The lows remind me of what truly matters. The lows remind me to be grateful. The lows remind me of who I am and who I am not. And the highs become a celebration of overcoming the lows. Of having loved ones to be able to give love back to the same way they showed me when I needed them.

I would not have these people in my life if I first didn't have the courage to be myself.

I believe it is important to be honest with yourself but also with those you love. Often we realise how we are feeling simply by having someone in our life hold space for us. Sometimes we need that mirror of support to acknowledge the truth of how we are feeling.

What have you given up in order to fit in? Your values, ideals, hopes, dreams, desires? Even if we don't think we do it, we all do it to some capacity. Due to society and conditioning we automatically fall into this without realising. Which is exactly why a true sense of belonging feels so challenging. Ultimately, we try to fit in in order to belong. But too often we sacrifice what makes us, us!

What does belonging mean to you? What would it mean to you to truly feel like you were accepted and belonged?

How willing are you to have the tough conversations? To ask the person you've been dating where it's heading? To say you love someone first? To tell someone that you feel hurt by something that they did? To be the first to say sorry and that you were wrong?

Courage to me means being willing to get hurt. When my single friends tell me that they are done with being hurt by guys my response is, do you think that you don't get hurt being in a relationship?

I believe that when we open our heart, it can ache with love, but it can also ache with pain. I know I am ready to be in a relationship when I feel strong enough to ache for both. Relationships are going to be tough. I am probably going to cry all kinds of tears regardless of what kind of relationship I am in, because anything and everything can make me cry when I deeply love and care about someone. So it's not a matter of being in pain or not, but who am I willing to be in pain for? Who am I willing to cry for? Who am I willing to ache for? Who am I willing to be vulnerable for?

At the end of the day, deep down, we all just want to be loved, accepted and appreciated for who we are. No more, no less.

Dropping your defences is not the same as dropping your boundaries.
~ Richard Rudd

Brené Brown also says *it's much easier for us to project hurt than it is for us to feel our own pain.* When we shut ourselves off from ourselves we shut ourselves off from being able to deeply feel others. To be able to go where no one has been willing to ever go with them. To sometimes go where they themselves haven't been willing to go. It's like when someone asks how you are and you just start crying because you just feel that they can hold you in your emotions and that it's safe to break in front of them. We can only hold this for others, this safe space to truly be all that we are, when we learn to first hold it for ourselves. It simply comes down to our level of courage and self-responsibility of owning our emotions.

For the Entrepreneur…

People pleasing. *Sigh* Although I feel I have come a long way, this is a constant work in progress. Every time I'm faced with disappointing someone I love and wanting to help them but also doing what's right for me, it takes so much courage to do what I feel is the right thing in that situation. I really had to consciously decide not to feel guilty for not doing what they wanted or expected me to. Every situation is different and unique but what determines my decision pretty much every time is my intuition. (I cover this more in the chapter on Intuition.)

Especially as my business grew to multi-six figures I had demands, expectations, opportunities and offers left, right and centre. There is definitely no shortage of options. No shortage of what I want to do. No shortage of what matters. But it becomes more about prioritising my time, focusing my attention and having clear boundaries with saying no to most things in order to stay on track with the direction I'm already moving in.

A good friend of mine Kresant says – *If it's not a f*** yes, it's a f*** no!*

The truth is it's easy to say yes to everyone. It's easy to say yes to every social gathering, every event, every book, every conversation, every training and every course.

But every time I say yes to something I'm saying no to a hundred others.

When I say yes to investing my most precious resource (my time) it's taking time away from something else that I value more – family, time alone, creating.

It takes more courage to say no than it does to say yes. And it takes even more courage to continually say no, no, no and no again. Temptation doesn't necessarily get easier. But you become stronger. But as we get stronger, so do the challenges we are confronted by!!

Belonging in business comes from being unapologetically you.

For entrepreneurs, to feel like we belong, we need to stop trying to be everything to everyone. We must find our tribe where we can fully be accepted, for all that we are.

If you are craving a heart-centred community of other like-minded people where you can feel empowered, supported, vulnerable, safe, with sense of belonging, where we promote collaboration over competition, head to www.TheNakedYouBook.com/Resources or follow me on Instagram @ NinaTheNakedCoach where I also share details about my community.

Presence

The presence you give a person when you listen to them
gives them that space to be ok to be
It gives them the permission
To feel how it feels just to be

Don't you also want that
Just to love and feel loved
So the best thing you can do for someone
Is listen, be present and love

As when someone isn't present
They are not allowing you the space
It's just more difficult
To hug without a mutual embrace

So when you CHOOSE to hug
Hug with arms wide open
Or don't hug at all
Until you have learnt
It's ok to feel completely broken

~ Nina Concepcion

CHAPTER 10

Answering The Call

CHAPTER 10

Answering The Call

Who wants to be a leader anyway?

I remember thinking this over and over again when I was going through a bit of an identity crisis just before I fell pregnant! I was so unwilling to be honest with what I was being called to step into. I think we start by believing we chose something out of what we want, like a goal or a career. Then we realise that it chose us. That we cannot unchoose it with a snap of our fingers.

Almost every superhero movie I can think of undergoes the same story line, *chose someone else, I didn't choose this*. The thing is, I believe we did. I believe our soul did. Which is why our logical minds try to control this choice. Of course we can choose not to follow the calling, but I think this is when we start to feel those nudges of intuition get stronger and stronger until life slaps us right in the face.

I've come to believe that rather than being a leader by choice, true leaders are born out of a necessity, a need. They just seem to have a little bit more courage to do what most people are not willing to do. When they are faced with doing the right thing or pointing the responsibility at someone else, it's almost as if there seems to be no other option but to help. They aren't going to wait around and HOPE for someone else to do it. Even though they "didn't choose it". When push comes to shove, they show up.

It's easy to ignore problems when you are ignorant, blind or unaware.

But once you see, you cannot unsee.

Once you discover a fight truly worth fighting, is it even plausible to consider another option? Does there become any other option but to speak up when you see wrong doing, to stand up for a person who has no voice, to stop harm from happening to an innocent child?

I can't expect anyone to stand with me, to speak up with me, to march with me.

However, I admire those who do!

It takes courage.

Strength.

I'm not saying I am these things.

I'm saying I've had to grow INTO these things.

The truth is we are all courageous and strong. We just forget. We're just conditioned otherwise. We've just allowed our minds to be redirected. Most of us just don't give ourselves the opportunity to prove it to ourselves.

So yes we are courageous. We are strong.

Let's remember this. Let's take action. Let's embody this.

Not merely for ourselves. But for what's needed. For change to occur. For a deeper connection with humanity.

We often don't speak up because we don't want to make a scene. We don't want to cause trouble. We don't want to seem crazy.

But if that's the RESULT of needing to speak up, share our truth, uphold our values, will we have the courage to do what's needed?

Are we willing to do what is hard and necessary or what's easy and convenient?

Let's not fight for the sake of fighting. But when something is worth and needs fighting for, we mustn't be scared of what's required of us to play our part.

Why is it so easy for us to overlook our magnificence, and yet we can see it so clearly in others?

Just as easily as it is for us to be selfish and just think of ourselves, until someone we love is hurt, instantly within a split second, we become selfless and are able to give from an infinite pool we hadn't even known existed until that moment of need!

It's not just about what you do but about how your impact impacts us all. We will likely never witness the entire ripple effect. The same way that our mentors who do and don't know of us, will likely never grasp the ripple impact they have and are making. But we can choose and feel to believe.

For more free resources in how to answer your calling head to www.TheNakedYouBook.com/Resources

~ Journal on the questions below ~

QUESTIONS
- What has been calling you?
- Is there something I am running away from?

CHAPTER 11

Transformation

CHAPTER 11

Transformation

Butterfly

*I had to lose who I was
to discover the me right now
I had to let it all go
not knowing the next step or how*

*everything I thought I was
everything I once loved so much
all packed up in boxes
not even desiring to touch*

*space is what I needed
to just think about me again
to not think of other people
and to not condemn*

for putting myself first
and taking care of me
I had neglected myself
and was just too busy to see

I was making myself sick
running myself to the ground
not doing enough I would say
repeating to myself that sound

but it woke me up
a change had to be made
there wasn't anything else
I was willing to trade

I do want kids one day
I'm not willing to sacrifice
So, goodbye guilt
there's no need to analyse

I did feel like a failure
I cried and cried so much
but deep down I just knew
concerns would just go hush hush

it definitely tested my faith in the universe having my back
but she's never let me down
she's led me down the right track

so I kept blind faith
keeping those I love close by
only doing what I love
has kept my head held high

I didn't know what was next
I didn't know who I was
and yet the people I love reminded me
of exactly who I was

I wasn't changing
just my truest expression
parts of me
we're growing more extensions

"I know you're doing what's best for you
and I'm so proud of you"
a reminder that nothing needs to change
be patience and you'll see your cue

I was always on track even though I felt unsure
but it's exactly what I needed
if it sounds sane or obscure

I've learned to love myself again
regardless of who I am or what I do
I've learnt to accept myself
for my mishaps too

for my overly loud laugh
and sometimes jumping the gun
for laughing at stupid shit
or just being myself for fun

I've learned not everybody will like me
and that's okay
I've learnt we just trigger some people
for doing nothing except being in their day

I've learned it's not entirely about the money or the
stresses going on
but about your inner strength
and your will to carry on

it's about your mindset and the knowing
"it's not that big of a deal, I can figure this out"
I'll be ok
I have no doubt

I have shelter, food, clothes, and connection
there are not many other needs for objections

I'm putting food on the table
surrounded by love of laughing
with people I love
that's all I really need to be standing

I'm still getting out of debt
I still don't have any savings
and yet I'm loving my life
and enjoying the simple engravings

if I'm having fun
and choosing what's right for me
it will all work out
I can now again see

the transformation is happening
I'm about to leap and fly
as something a new
with the same blue sky

I'm being rewarded again
for listening to my intuition
dancing I am
I'm my life's musician

~ Nina Concepcion

What if, before we call anything in, there is something we must first release?

It's easy for us to complain about our current situation and wish for it to be different. But we often overlook the cons, what's required of us and the sacrifices made once we have that thing we say we want.

I've spoken to hundreds of coaches globally who want to hit their next record month. But it's not until they do, that many of them don't learn to appreciate what they had in abundance, before they got really busy. Before they hit their record month. We get so concerned with what we want that we often miss the gifts in the present moment.

Before the record month even happens, there is normally some form of energetic release that happens in order to make more space for what we want to attract. This normally always includes tears, feelings of wanting to give up and getting triggered. It's not until we can release an old part of our thinking, an old belief, our identity, our fear or what we think we should be doing, where space opens up for exactly what we're calling in.

Just yesterday I gave this analogy to one of my high-level clients.

I feel like you're carrying all this luggage that doesn't serve you. The universe is trying to give you more but your hands are full. If you take on any more you'll feel like you will want to burst as you're ready overwhelmed. How can you let go of what you think you need and trust the process? How can you trust that when you let go of this, something better will be on its way? How can you have faith in the universe?

Are you willing to let go of needing to please everyone? Are you willing to step away from your safe hiding place? Are you willing to allow death to happen, to be reborn? Or will you let fear stop you?

The truth is when it's feeling uncomfortable and you've already taken the first step... You're ALREADY in the thick of it. If you stop and turn back it's the same distance as if you just kept going! All you need to do is trust, breathe, let go, and keep going.

The moment we feel we don't have to have it all figured out is the moment of opportunity where we can let go of the expectation that it's us that must do everything.
~ Nina Concepcion

During the process of writing this book... I felt as if a transformation was occurring. To be honest it felt similar to being pregnant! Getting started was relatively easy, the second trimester was the smoothest then the third trimester was the most challenging and triggering. I felt like I was giving birth to a new version of myself. A more embodied unapologetic version of myself.

We often say we want transformation, growth, progress, but we often forget what is asked of us, required of us... in order for that transformation to occur. If we want to receive more, we must give more. There is no receiver without a giver. We must be willing to give AND receive more.

It can be painful, confronting, uncomfortable and vulnerable. We literally feel naked when we have nothing left to hide behind.

But are you willing to strip yourself bare? Are you willing to stand there naked, without any layers, masks or illusions? Do you have the courage to trust yourself? To trust the universe, a higher power that you are taken care of?

Will you lean in? Or will you run away? Will you embrace when you feel uncomfortable and learn to love yourself through the pain and transformation, or are you expecting someone else to come in and save you?

When I am struggling to lean in… When I am summoning up the courage to tap into a new level of strength… I remind myself…

What is a butterfly, after it is the caterpillar but before it becomes the butterfly?

We often forget about the PROCESS of transformation. While we are transitioning, we are between worlds. We are a big ball of mess.

In the case of a caterpillar and butterfly this is actually called a chrysalis. A chrysalis is a transitional state between two developmental stages of the SAME species. Many of us are undergoing a transformation. To be more precise many of us are undergoing MANY transformations. You may find yourself in the midst of one while reading this book. It truly is no accident that you are here now. Out of anywhere in the world you can be, you are here with me in spirit.

Did you know that the word "coincidence" actually means to perfectly align. It does not mean "accident".

Can you see these synchronicities happening around you? Are you paying attention to the signs? Are you asking and seeking support?

Challenge is the opposite of ease. Many of us want transformation but we are unwilling to let go of the old and allow a death to occur.

Struggle is a natural part of growth. For our muscles as humans, for the wings of a butterfly, for us and our evolution! Did you know that if you actually help a butterfly break through its chrysalis, without it experiencing the struggle, the butterfly would never fly because it needs to push through the cocoon itself to build the strength to fly?

Many of us are out there trying to "save" people. I get it, because I used to feel like I wanted to save people all the time. It hurt me to see other people hurt. These are common traits I see with my fellow empaths and coaches who are starting out in business. I have come to realise that... similar to the butterfly...

> *When you save someone, you rob them off the opportunity*
> *of discovering the gift of saving themselves.*
> ~ Nina Concepcion

When we come to the rescue we are implying that we don't believe they can do it alone. It doesn't mean we don't help. It means that the best way to empower them is to give people an opportunity to help themselves by guiding and supporting them, and instead of sweeping in from a deep seeded insecurity and of not feeling good enough.

Thoughts, I've had to continually remind myself and my clients of during times of challenge are:

- If I wasn't ready for this, I wouldn't have been attracted it
- What's the lesson in this?
- A new challenge means another level is just on the other side.
- As plant medicine reminded me – I'm stronger than I think I am!

What if I just want to be in flow all the time?

A distinct finding for me is just because we can have a meaningful life with ease and flow, it doesn't mean we won't encounter resistance. It doesn't mean it will be comfortable. It doesn't mean we won't have fears to face. We all have conditioning to overcome, we all have fears to test our resilience, we all attract experiences to learn what we need to evolve. Evolution requires a death of what we know, for something new to be reborn. Scott Oldford and I also spoke about this on our Interview for this book.

I believe it was Tony Robbins who said *our ability to stay congruent with who we are is the strongest human driver*. So if we believe ourselves to be unworthy, we will do anything (unconsciously and consciously) to stay consistent with this belief. To shift our actions long term, require a shift in our identity.

One of my biggest teachers has been plant medicine. I interviewed one of my mentors Jeffrey Slayter on this topic. Medicine reminds us of who we are, what it means to face ourselves. The spirits remind us what it means to be human, to feel, to be open, to be one.

For the full-length interview with Jeffrey Slayter or Scott Oldford go to www.TheNakedYouBook.com/Resources

It's Begun

The hurts still there
it's still dug deep
but what I can feel
is awakening in its sleep

the healing is starting
the rebuilding has begun
what was once overwhelming
is almost but not exactly numb

it's not as intense
every time I think
I can relive it
and not begin to sink

I can see the wounds
I can see the blood
I'm still in it
getting messy in the mud

but it no longer stings
to an unbearable cry
I can now start to see
a new found high

I can see the rainbow
in the gloomy storm
it's turning around
and starting to transform

I'm spreading my wings
I'm starting to fly
who knew it was possible
to not understand
how or why

time really does start to heal wounds
only if you don't allow yourself to be consumed

feel the pain but don't linger too long
focus on the light
and not where you went wrong

look at the lessons and grow with each pain
because hidden within it
is a lot more
for you to gain

~ Nina Concepcion

CHAPTER 12

Money and Meaning

CHAPTER 12

Money and Meaning

When the impossibility of replacing a person is realized,
it allows the responsibility which a man has for his existence
and his continuance, to appear in all its magnitude
~ Victor Frankl

Think of one person who has made a big impact on your life. It's hard to imagine your life without that person right? If you are reading this book, I can pretty much guarantee that the same can be said for you. There is someone who you have impacted in your life - that you have made a difference to. They may or may not have told you. One of the challenges with being an entrepreneur is that we don't often get the feedback or recognition for our work as fast as we would want it. We often question our value and our ability to make a difference especially if we are comparing ourselves to people like Tony Robbins or Oprah Winfrey.

Rather than focusing on the number of people I can help, I do my best to hone my focus on the person who is sitting in front of me right now. In the case of me writing this book, the people who are going to be reading this. My secret is that rather than looking for that validation externally, I look for the internal signs. How does this make me feel? Do I feel like I am authentically expressing myself through my work? Do I feel like I get to be me or am I holding myself back?

When I speak on stages and I am my crazy, loud, quirky self, able to laugh at myself and allow myself to cry, it doesn't matter how many people I am speaking to, I am proud of the way I am showing up.

Our job is to simply be us, shine our light and inspire others to do the same. Tony Robbins said something like, *I never endeavoured to be a business owner. But I realised having my own business was one of the most impactful ways to generate money to be able to make a bigger difference.*

People will not buy from you until they feel seen, heard and understood. Our first job, before offering anything, is to seek to understand each customer.
~ Nina Concepcion

That day my life changed…

When I saw Brendon Burchard speak for the first time… I had no ambition of having my own business. I just wanted to make "a" difference the same way he did for me. Brendon made me feel seen and understood in a way I had never experienced before. Even though I was one person in a crowd, I felt like he was speaking directly to me, to my soul. It felt more intimate than most one-on-one conversations I had ever had. I didn't know it was possible to feel that way.

When I finally gave myself permission to believe in something new, to believe my life could be bigger than my circumstances and my past… When I started to believe I was worthy of more… is when my reality started to reflect that back to me. Through the people, experiences and abundance that I attracted.

How can YOU give yourself permission to do something that you maybe have never allowed yourself to do before? Something you maybe didn't know was possible?

When he shared his story and spoke about his challenges, vulnerabilities and lessons. Tears streamed down my face as something inside me awoke. Something I didn't even know was there.

A vision I didn't even know I had!

I sat there crazily writing notes in my notebook with my new realisation… *I can actually make a difference sharing my story just like Brendon! Real estate is only temporary… I'm here to be a coach, speaker and author just like Brendon! If he can do it. So can I!!!*

When we outgrow our current situation, when our reality no longer reflects our standards, it becomes impossible to not take any action to move into that next version of ourselves. The reason for this, is that doing nothing at this point in your journey actually seems more painful than taking action (doing something unknown).

My thought was, I can be just like Brendon! NOT Brendon. But me.

Even if I could empower just ONE person the way Brendon had impacted me on that day, I knew my life would make a real difference. This book is a ripple effect of that day.

Money is an exchange of services that have been demanded,
that you can supply more effectively and efficiently,
at a reasonable price, more than anyone, CONSISTENTLY…
You can't expect to excel in something that's not truly one of your
highest values.
~ Dr John Demartini

THIS is Step 1 in what causes an entrepreneur to become wealthy. During my interview with Dr Demartini he made me realise that wealth was not high enough on my priorities for it to become a reality for me. Wealth needs to be in your top one or two values in order for you to attain it. Dr Demartini was pivotal in supporting me in shifting and aligning my values to make the next two years the most successful years in my business that I have ever had, to date.

So when you think about what you desire in life and business why is it that you truly desire it? Does this align with your values?

John's last piece of advice was:

Don't compare yourself to others. Compare your daily actions with
your own highest values and dreams. Delegate all your lower priority
activities,
with people who are inspired to do those.
Go out, serve people, get paid to do this,
so that you can help the economy and engage other people's lives.

If you would like access to watch or listen to the video interview with Dr John Demartini and for more support on having a more empowered story around money head to www.TheNakedYouBook.com/Resources.

CHAPTER 13

A New Beginning

CHAPTER 13

A New Beginning

We come to the end of this book.

But rather than being the end this can be a new start to your journey. To your next journey.

Dr John Demartini's last words he wanted to leave us with at the end of my interview with him was this:

Give yourself permission to be your authentic self. Have the courage to be yourself. The courage to be you, is the greatest courage you can ever have.
We cannot make a difference when we are conforming, but instead when we are individualised….

Here are the last journaling questions I have for you:
- What was the biggest thing I learnt about myself throughout this book?
- What am I going to make my life mean now?
- What is important to me in life and business?
- What must I do to embrace my imperfection?
- How will this impact the quality of my life and business?
- What are the words I would like to feel every day of my life and how can I honour myself whilst cultivating these?

It has truly been my pleasure and honour being here with you… For me the journey isn't over, it has just begun!

Thank you for taking the time to be with me, to be with you and to question your role in humanity and the collective. Hopefully one day we can meet in person and I can give you a big hug! In the meantime I am sending you a big virtual energetic hug!

I love you and appreciate you.

If you would like to share your experience with me and this book please send us an email or leave a review/comment at the www.TheNakedYouBook.com/contact I would love to hear how what you have taken away from our time together :)

If you don't want our journey to end (I know that I don't want it to end) and you would still like some support including:
- Access to a supportive heart-centred community
- *The Naked You: Online Course*
- Coaching/Mentorship
- Becoming a coach or making a full time six-figure income as a coach

including my signature program *Conscious Coaching 101*
- "Conscious Sales" Training or Courses
- How to discover how to tap into your own authentic expression through service (a business)
- Or if you simply would like some support but you are unsure of what support you need…

Please head to www.TheNakedYouBook.com/Resources and one of my team members will connect with you to explore what support you need and direct you to the best people for what you are after :)

To access any of the free resources mentioned in this book including free resources, gifts, bonus, exclusive interview access head to www.TheNakedYouBook.com/Resources

The last thing I will leave you with for now, is one of my favourite poems I have written. I wrote this back in 2015, six years prior to having this book published. I wrote it on a mountain in Bali where I "randomly" found my name carved into a wall! It was the first time I had truly felt at home.

I believe that you too…

Have started the journey home ♥

My Mantra

What's the point of resentment
What's the point of pain
When there's only really love and gratitude to be gained

Reflection of our inner self
The world that we create
Everyone is us
Just another way remade

Pain and holding on
often always only holds us back
from loving ourselves
down every single track

the path and journeys we attract
we experience
is really only testing our wants, desires and resilience

our desire to want to grow
into more of what we are
this lifetime
will you be a star or scar

treat every person with
gratitude and acceptance for exactly where they are
they are just parts of you reflected
interesting or bizarre

treat every living thing with respect and appreciation
as everything is just a reminder by an abbreviation

but the puzzles you see
are only for those who seek
if you are ready
you'll see congruency between the one being all unique

look at every experience as something to reveal
there's nothing that can ever be taken to steal

it is all you
everything is one
everything needs doing
at the same time everything is done

no need to feel guilty
because they are only you
put yourself first
because it true to do

responding to every experience with love, understanding,
that, how you respond
could cause or reverse your expanding

to consciously create experience
to become what is
remember it is everything
you can choose or choose not to dismiss

pay attention to the little things
and hold onto anger
or be the awakened
you are the dance not the dancer

~ Nina Concepcion

With all my love

Nina Concepcion xx

Follow & Connect with me on Instagram @NinaTheNakedCoach

About The Author

Nina Concepcion is the founder of "Conscious Sales". She is a "Conscious Sales" Coach, Mentor and Trainer supporting ambitious, heart-centred, coaches and entrepreneurs in building their business online from scratch to multi-six figures. She has ten years of experience in sales including two successful years in real estate where she became the youngest female top five sales earners in the company at the age of 22. She has used her high level of skills, experience and training in generating the same results to the conscious community as this is where her passion truly lies. She built her business to six figures through completely organic social media methods without paying for ads. And she has built her business to a quarter of a million dollars in 14 months.

She is also a speaker, online trainer and published author of her book *The Naked You: A Guide to Embracing Your Imperfections in Life and Business* which has earned her the name "The Naked Coach".

You can follow Nina on Instagram @NinaTheNakedCoach or head to www.TheNakedYouBook.com/Nina for more info.

www.ingramcontent.com/pod-product-compliance
Lightning Source LLC
Chambersburg PA
CBHW072149090426
42740CB00012B/2201